THE ART OF
ELEGANT
WOOD
KITCHENWARE

THE ART OF
ELEGANT
WOOD
KITCHENWARE

By Tony Lydgate

Sterling Publishing Co., Inc. New York
A Sterling/Chapelle Book

FOR CHAPELLE LTD.

Owner
Jo Packham

Editor
Cherie Hanson

Staff
Malissa Boatwright • Rebecca Christensen
Holly Fuller • Amber Hansen
Holly Hollingsworth • Susan Jorgensen
Susan Laws • Amanda McPeck
Barbara Milburn • Leslie Ridenour
Cindy Rooks • Cindy Stockel
Ryanne Webster • Nancy Whitley

Photography
Kevin Dilley for
Hazen Photography

Styling
Cherie Herrick

Illustrations
Richard Long

Library of Congress Cataloging-in Publication Data Available

Lydgate, Tony.
    The art of elegant wood kitchenware / by Tony Lydgate.
        p.   cm.
    "A Sterling/Chapelle book."
    Includes index.
    ISBN 0-8069-3888-9
    1. Woodwork. 2. Kitchen utencils. I. Title.
TT200.L93   1995
674'. 88—dc20   95-37041
                                               CIP

1 3 5 7 9 10 8 6 4 2
Published by Sterling Publishing Company, Inc.
387 Park Avenue South, New York, N.Y. 10016
© 1996 by Chapelle Ltd.
Distributed in Canada by Sterling Publishing
℅ Canadian Manda Group, One Atlantic Avenue, Suite 105
Toronto, Ontario, Canada M6K 3E7
Distributed in Great Britain and Europe by Cassell PLC
Wellington House, 125 Strand, London WC2R 0BB, England
Distributed in Australia by Capricorn Link (Australia) Pty Ltd.
P.O. Box 6651, Baulkham Hills, Business Center, NSW 2153, Australia
Printed and bound in Hong Kong
All rights reserved

Sterling ISBN 0-8069-3888-9

CONTENTS

Since prehistoric times, humankind has used wooden utensils for preparing and serving food. The ready availability of wood, the ease with which it can be worked into an endless variety of useful shapes, and perhaps even its affinity with fire have all made it an ideal material. Food-related utensils were among the primary wooden products of the early toolmaker's art, and the ones celebrated in this book are the direct descendants of these ancient originals.

Practical and simple, sculptural or complex, utensils make excellent projects for woodworkers at all skill levels, from beginner to expert. This book presents more than 75 designs by 34 of America's leading utensil makers. From the simplest chopstick to the most stunning bowl, each project gives the reader the means — as well as the inspiration — to become part of humankind's oldest woodworking tradition.

Although the basic form of a spoon, bowl, board or stirrer is easily recognizable, no two are exactly alike. Utensils can be made in an infinite number of shapes, and as the pages that follow illustrate, the woodworkers who make them have a ready opportunity to express their own individual vision. All projects are designed to be made in the home workshop, and are intended solely for personal use, and not for commercial manufacture or sale. Beginning utensil makers will benefit from explanations of some of the tricks of the trade; the skilled will enjoy seeing which of their many secrets are explained, and which are left to be discovered.

Carving Set by Karl Schroen

CREATING BY SUBTRACTING

Unlike jewelry boxes or furniture, which typically are constructed by adding together a number of smaller components, many utensils are created by subtraction. Through carving, sanding, or lathe turning, portions of the original wood are removed, revealing the utensil inside. In this sense, utensil making relies on the techniques and approaches associated with traditional sculpture. Several of the woodworkers quoted in the text describe the pleasure of visualizing the finished utensil inside the raw wood, where it lies hiding, and the delight they feel in watching as they allow that form gradually to emerge.

Carving, sander shaping, and lathe turning are the main methods by which the subtractive projects in this book are created. Although the instructions for each give an overview of the tools and techniques used, a thorough presenta-

tion of these methods is beyond the scope of this book. Instead, the reader is referred to Sterling Publishing's many books on carving and the lathe, available at your local bookstore and library, as well as to Tony Lydgate's *The Art of Making Elegant Wood Boxes*, and *Award Winning Boxes: Design and Technique*, which contain useful sections on sanding. In addition, several of the utensil makers featured in these pages have also published how-to books.

Another important source of information is to seek out and learn from skilled utensil makers, many of whom exhibit at local craft shows, or at the national exhibitions sponsored by the American Craft Council.

Bowl by Judy Ditmer

Bowl by Phil Payne

No matter where you live, ideal wood for utensils is all around you, as the trees that grow on the streets and in the backyard yield beautiful lumber. Moreover, grain patterns such as burl, birdseye, crotch, curly or fiddleback appear in these species as frequently as in more familiar woods. For some projects, a trip to a commercial lumberyard may be in order. Make sure that any wood you buy came from a source that is certified to practice sustainable yield forest management.

WHAT WOODS TO USE

One of the great pleasures of utensil making is using "found" wood. With their small size and often irregular, organic shapes, utensils allow their makers to take advantage of something many woodshops accumulate: interesting, odd-shaped pieces of wood that are too small to use, but too nice to throw away. The lumber for many of the beautiful objects in this book was salvaged from rejects, castoffs, and discards. In addition to collecting the warped boards, crooked logs, and curly butts that furniture makers and cabinet shops are forced to abandon, the utensil makers in this book obtain their raw material from surprising sources. Barry Gordon, the master spoonmaker whose work is shown beginning on page 34, raids his firewood pile, while bowlmakers Phil Payne (page 29) and Marc Gardner (page 75) chase after the highway department's tree-trimming crew and the developer's bulldozer.

Servers by Barry Gordon

Vertizontal by Dennis Elliott

A NOTE ABOUT POWER TOOLS

Some woodworkers prefer to use the carver's handheld axes and adzes, gouges and chisels, rasps, rifflers and files. Others create their work using power tools. Particularly for cutting boards, salt shakers and other projects that involve assembling parts to construct a larger whole, common woodworking tools such as the table saw and belt sander are a necessity. For a table saw, a l0" blade diameter is the most practical, and heavier-duty models are preferable because they tend to be more accurate, especially for repeated cuts. A sturdy fence and adjustable miter fence are essential accessories. Saw blades should be carbide-tipped, and kept as sharp as possible. Kerf width, number and type of teeth vary according to the particular cut to be made. Blades accumulate resin, especially when milling dense hardwoods; after each hour of use, clean them with spray-on oven cleaner. With this and all power tools, always read, understand and follow manufacturer's instructions.

Once you have selected a piece of beautiful wood, the grain-enhancing shine of its finished surfaces is produced mainly by sanding. Sandpaper consists of a jumble of tiny rocks glued to a paper or cloth backing. These rocks engrave a pattern of grooves, like furrows plowed into a field, on the wood they are applied to. When a belt sander is used, these grooves are parallel and of uniform depth. How deep is determined by the grit rating of the abrasive: as this number increases, groove depth decreases. A perfect finish is produced by repeated sanding with progressively finer grits, making these parallel grooves shallower and shallower until they become effectively invisible.

It is important to follow an orderly sequence of grits. Too broad a leap, such as going from coarse to very fine with nothing in between, does not work: trying to remove 60-grit scratches with a 220-grit abrasive will simply produce well-sanded scratches, for the 220x rocks are too small to obliterate the grooves the 60x rocks have made. A 6" x 48" stationary belt sander is the basic sanding tool used to flatten and smooth irregular surfaces, clean up dried glue and newspaper, and give a project its basic shape.

Other useful abrasive power tools are the vibrator or orbital sander, the pneumatic drum sander, sanding cylinders or sleeves that can be mounted on a rotating shaft or drill press, and inflatable bladder or flap-wheel sanders. A small handheld router, power carving wheel or similar Dremel-type tool is often used to remove material from small areas, especially concave spaces.

Many utensils possess curved shapes, and the band saw is one of the best tools for creating these forms from rough lumber. For larger projects such as bowls, a chain saw is used to rough-hew a bowl blank from a log or tree stump. The blank is then mounted on a lathe, one of the most versatile woodshop tools, which was used to produce many of the projects in this book. Excellent introductions to the lathe, and other guides and instruction books on lathes and wood turning are available from your local bookstore and library, or a good woodworking supply store or catalog.

Cutting Board by Al Ladd

LAMINATING CUTTING BOARDS

The technique for making cutting boards, a type of lamination, involves gluing pieces of wood together on edge. Use a thickness planer or sander to make certain all parts are of uniform thickness. Mill one edge perfectly straight with a joiner, and then rip each piece to appropriate width on a table saw. To glue up the laminate or cutting board, use clean scrap lumber to make a "sandwich" clamping jig. In addition to clamping the edges, keep the assembly being glued from buckling by sandwiching it between two pairs of blocks, clamped over the face of the assembly on either end.

To avoid gluing the clamping blocks to the cutting board — or the cutting board to the work table — line each block with a single sheet of newspaper. The glue won't penetrate the newspaper, which means that when it is dry and the clamps are removed, everything should come apart easily. The newspaper is then sanded off, along with the excess dried glue.

Goblets by Betty Scarpino

ADHESIVES AND FINISHES

Since most of the projects in this book are designed to come in contact with water, only waterproof adhesives should be used. Aliphatic resins, two-part epoxies and other appropriate adhesives are readily available at hardware stores or through woodworking supply stores or catalogs. For all wood utensils, exposure to water should be minimized whenever possible. To clean, wash by hand in mild soap and water, and do not allow a glued utensil to soak overnight. Use of an automatic dishwasher exposes the wood to sustained extreme heat, which is harmful.

Since utensils also come in contact with food, the many varieties of varnish, lacquer and penetrating oil commonly used on boxes and furniture are unsuitable. Instead, utensil finishes must be edible and nontoxic. Mineral oil and preparations containing walnut or other natural oils and waxes are the most widely used. An additional advantage of such oil finishes is that they can be renewed as needed by re-oiling. Contact with water tends to raise the grain of hardwood, and after washing, the surface of some utensils may take on a slightly furry appearance and feel. To minimize this in his cutting boards, Ed Wohl (page 70) twice-dips each piece in water to raise the grain, allows it to dry, and then sands it smooth again before oiling.

SAFETY

Woodworking is inherently dangerous. The raw material itself can be heavy, sharp-edged and splintery, and the tools used to fabricate it are all potentially lethal. These factors, combined with noxious dust, harmful chemicals, high noise levels and large quantities of electricity, produce an environment in which injuries can occur in dozens of unforeseen ways. To operate a safe woodshop, always keep this in mind. The risk of injury can never be completely removed, but it can be reduced to an acceptable level by strict observation of the following guidelines:

1. For safe operation of table saw, lathe and other power tools, make certain that you read, understand and adhere to manufacturer's instructions.

2. Never allow fingers to come near any moving blade or cutter. Use a push stick.

3. When using handheld carving tools, keep your hands out of the path of the tool. Make sure the workpiece is securely held in place.

4. Always wear a respirator or dust mask in the shop. Always wear eye and ear protection when using power tools.

5. Wear appropriate clothing. A heavy work apron will protect the lap and midsection, and proper footwear will soften the impact of the occasional dropped log or chisel.

6. Never perform any operation without being satisfied that you understand it and are comfortable with it.

7. Keep your mind on your work. Do not allow your attention to wander, especially when performing repetitive operations.

8. Never work when you are tired, in a hurry, or simply not in the mood to work. It is better to stop, or find something to do outside the shop for a while. Return refreshed and in the proper frame of mind.

BOWLS

NATURAL EDGE BOWL
GENE BUSCHER

The Natural Edge Bowl (above) and the Koa Serving Bowl (page 16) are shaped on a spindle carver, which consists of a 3-foot metal shaft with a high-speed steel blade on one end. The inside surfaces are smoothed with a handheld grinder, then sanded and oiled with mineral oil.

GENE BUSCHER

Gene Buscher was trained as a draftsman, but decided to take up woodworking when he left his native California to live on the big island of Hawaii. "I had a carver friend who let me be his apprentice, and he showed me how to do the kind of carving I use to make my bowls."

Gene follows the natural form of whatever piece of wood he uses. "I don't like trying to invent a shape. For me the challenge is to let the natural material tell me what it wants me to do. On some of my bowls, I leave the edges raw, just like they came from the log." The bowls shown here are made of koa, a species of hardwood native to Hawaii. Both have exceptional curly figure, also called fiddleback or tigertail.

None of the wood for Gene's bowls is cut from living trees. "I harvest all my material by hand from stumps or branches that are already down on the ground. It's really more like salvage work." In addition to koa, Gene also uses other Hawaiian woods such as milo, kou, sandalwood, robusta, mango, and lichee nut.

KOA SERVING BOWL
GENE BUSCHER

Photo by Bob Barrett

JUDY DITMER

"I knew I was an artist when I was four years old, but it took me a long time to find my medium," Judy Ditmer says. As one of the country's leading woodturners, and author, Judy's persistence has clearly paid off.

"As a child, I always liked to make things, and to take things apart and figure out how they work. I never got much encouragement, though, even when I went to art school, and I'd about given up on being able to do art for a living when I discovered wood turning. I happened to go to a conference on turning, and got just blown out of the water. 'This is it,' I thought to myself, 'this is what I've been looking for.'

"What I like about turning is that the design process and the making process are so integrated. You don't start with a paper-and-pencil drawing, then set out to build it. Instead, you're making decisions as you do the cutting. It's a subtractive process: the bowl is right there in the wood, waiting. When you reach that preexisting final form, there's such a sense of rightness."

MAPLE BOWL
JUDY DITMER

This simple but elegant round footed bowl is maple. Judy starts by chain sawing the bowl blank out of a log, then turning it while the unseasoned wood is still green. After proper air drying, the final form is turned and sanded, then oiled with mineral oil.

OCTAGONAL-RIMMED BOWL
JUDY DITMER

The eight-sided rim of this bowl shows the original shape of the bowl blank as it was chain-sawed from the maple log. Judy crosscuts a 12" section of log, then saws it in half in the direction of the grain. The four corners are then sliced off, leaving an eight-sided form. The blank is turned on the lathe while still green, and the straight sides of the blank are simply left on. After drying, the bowl is turned round and polished; the edges of the rim are sanded, and the bowl is oiled with mineral oil.

CURLY KOA BOWL
JACK STRAKA

The symmetrical round shape of this bowl indicates that it was turned on a lathe, rather than carved. The wood is turned in its green or unseasoned state. When dry, it is returned to the lathe, and the finishing touches — including these delicate, thin walls — are produced. Sanding and polishing the bowl while it is still on the lathe allows the brilliant curly grain to show when it is oiled with mineral oil.

JACK STRAKA

Jack Straka's electrical and mechanical training led to a successful career with a large corporation, where he supervised instrument manufacture. "The corporate culture was good to me when I was younger," Jack remembers, "but when I hit 40 I began to feel it was time for a big change." That change took him through the Caribbean to Hawaii, where he lives and works today.

"I was fortunate that when I started woodworking, I had enough savings to give me plenty of time to build my business up. I didn't have to pressure myself into doing anything. After all those years with the company, the laid-back style of Hawaii was exactly what I needed."

Jack was also fortunate in finding a local bowlmaker who turned out to be the perfect teacher. "Because of the Hawaiian tradition, bowls are a popular item here. I like the functionality of bowls, and with these beautiful native woods, it's hard to go wrong." Jack harvests logging rejects, and his favorite woods are mango, Norfolk pine, and koa.

"I think of all my pieces as utilitarian, but I know that some people use them just for decoration. Even though I turn the same basic shapes, since the wood varies so much, the way the differing grain shows up makes every one different."

BURLWOOD FRUIT BOWL
LLOYD GENERAL

22

LLOYD GENERAL

For many years, Lloyd General enjoyed a successful career as a master carpenter, until his doctor informed him in 1984 that his arthritis would get much worse if he didn't give up using a hammer. Since Lloyd had been trained as a machinist, he decided to explore wood turning as an alternative to carpentry, and bought his first lathe. "I was intending to make some stools as my first project," Lloyd remembers. "But I had some blocks of wood that looked like they'd make nice bowls, so I made them first, and now here I am!"

"I hate the thought of ever cutting down a tree," Lloyd says, "but once the wood is on the ground from storm windfalls or land clearing, let me at it!" He estimates he hauls 40 tons of logs each year to his Northern California shop, and he uses only native California species, particularly bay laurel and claro walnut.

"To me, there's nothing more fun than coming home with a load of logs on my truck, then winching them off and sawing them up into bowl blocks, getting it just the way you want it. When you study the wood, you can see how it tells you the tale of its life. You can see the annual rings, and the wide ones show you the years of flood in the valley. Before I start work, I look to see the finished bowl right there in the log."

All Lloyd's bowls are turned "green," that is, the wood has not been dried before it goes on the lathe. "Some days, I can go from harvested log to finished bowl before suppertime. Then as the wood dries over the next few weeks, the bowl will change shape. I love all that movement in the wood, the way the bowl turns irregular, takes on its own personality. I can't think of a better life than making one bowl at a time."

BURLWOOD FRUIT BOWL &
FIGURED CLARO WALNUT SALAD BOWL

These bowls begin as blocks chain-sawed from whole logs of green wood. The area of the block that will become the foot of the bowl is flattened, then attached to the faceplate of the lathe. After the bowl is turned, it is removed from the lathe and set aside to air-dry for two to four weeks. The shape of the bowl usually changes as the wood dries, warping or twisting. The natural irregularities this movement produces are one of the features that make Lloyd's bowls so pleasing to the eye.

After the wood is dry, the bowl is re-mounted on the lathe, and the interior and exterior surfaces are sanded with progressively finer sandpaper. The fact that the bowl is no longer perfectly spherical in shape can make this sanding process awkward. Once sanded, the bowl is oiled with any food-safe finish, such as mineral oil or olive oil.

FIGURED CLARO WALNUT SALAD BOWL
LLOYD GENERAL

Photo by Bob Barrett

HOLLY TORNHEIM

Holly Tornheim studied elementary education, planning to become a teacher after graduation. "My third year in college, I was part of a work-study construction project in the Sierra Nevada foothills. I found I really loved building things, and although I still volunteer in the schools, I've stayed a builder."

Holly continued to work as a carpenter until her daughter was born. "Having kids made it harder to be part of a construction crew, so I began looking for work closer to home," she says. Fortunately, she lived near Bob Erickson, one of the country's finest furniture makers. "Bob hired me as an apprentice, and his shop is where I learned fine woodworking."

"I got started on spoons and utensils because my daughter does marvellous watercolors. At age eight, she'd produced some greeting cards to sell at a local craft fair. I figured that if I was going to sit with her in a booth for a weekend, I might as well have something to sell myself, so I made some spoons.

"To make my utensils, I use all the shaping and sanding techniques I learned from Bob Erickson. I like not using patterns in my work. I never know how something is going to turn out: I just keep working on it until I'm pleased with how it looks."

GRATED CHEESE BOWL & SPOON SETS
HOLLY TORNHEIM

All of Holly Tornheim's pieces are shaped using a variety of sanding tools, including a handheld Dremel-type sander, a 1" belt sander, a 6" x 48" stationary belt sander, and lots of hand sanding. She uses a walnut oil finish, which polymerizes when dry.

Native California woods like manzanita, madrone and walnut, along with maple and exotics like granadillo and narra are used for the bowl-and-spoon sets. The spoons are made in the same way as Holly's Chopsticks (page 82) and her Spoon, Knife & Fork Set (page 49). The bowls begin as square chunks of wood; Holly band saws as much of the shape as possible, then uses carvers' gouges and sanding to create the final form.

SALT CELLARS
HOLLY TORNHEIM

NATURE'S NEVER-ENDING GIFT
PHIL PAYNE

PHIL PAYNE

"When I do something, I want it done right, that's just the way I am. It's not finished till I'm satisfied with it, and if I'm not satisfied with it, it don't go!" says Phil Payne, whose career as a wood-carver didn't begin until a mishap cut short his previous occupation as a tractor-trailer driver.

During his recovery, Phil began carving. "Both my father and grandfather built houses, and I've drawn all my life," Phil remembers. "I think the first spoon I ever carved was for my mother, on Mother's Day when I was six years old. Nowadays most of my work is functional; when I get away from the idea of using something is when I get what I call fancy."

Phil's spoons and bowls are highly prized for their natural shapes, which follow the grain of the wood. "I had a pine knot once, I stared at it for two years before I saw there was a Conquistador in it. My wife says she can see a bowl in a chunk of wood before I start to carve it, but most of the time, not me. I let the wood talk to me, I go with it," Phil says.

Phil's bowls begin as chain-sawed blocks of unseasoned, green wood. He roughs them out entirely by hand with an adze copied from a 16-century tool. A single 600-pound oak burl yielded him a total of 10 pieces, including "Nature's Never-Ending Gift" on the opposite page. "When I get through chopping," he says, "I've got a bowl!"

MACE'S GIFT
PHIL PAYNE
30

SALAD & DRESSING BOWL
WILLIAM CHAPPELOW & TOM REED
3 1

TRIPLE-SPOUTED SOUP TUREEN
WILLIAM CHAPPELOW & TOM REED
3 2

SPOONS, LADLES
& SUCH

CURLY MAPLE SALAD SERVERS
BARRY GORDON
3 4

Photo by Brantley Carroll

BARRY GORDON

Barry Gordon first became aware of wood carving as a young man, when a famous folk carver paid a visit to the small upstate New York town where he grew up. But like many of the craftspeople featured in this book, he wasn't bitten by the woodworking bug until some years afterward.

"I was pursuing a graduate degree in Geography when our second child was born," Barry remembers, "so I got to spend a lot of time at home with the kids, and I carved a few spoons. I've always enjoyed food and food preparation, and I've always liked tools, so I suppose it was inevitable that the two would come together. Then one day I took the kids and the spoons to the local Farmer's Market. I sold them all—the spoons, that is—and that was the beginning of the end of Geography."

All of Barry's spoons are made from woods that grow around Syracuse, New York, where he teaches spoon-making and manages the Eureka Crafts Gallery. Barry's favorite species is sugar maple. He buys rough-sawn lumber for some of his pieces, but many, especially the one-of-a-kind variety, come directly from the firewood pile. "I am the world's slowest firewood stacker," Barry acknowledges. "When my local firewood cutter brings me a cord, I go through the logs and look for likely candidates. It's not uncommon for me to start with a 40-pound log, and end up with one 8-ounce spoon."

Barry likes the fact that spoons are created by subtraction, by removing wood to release the utensil from where it lies hidden within the wood. Much of his work is functional, but he also enjoys making one-of-a-kind pieces that have their roots in traditional utensil forms but are clearly more like sculptural objects.

FIGURED MAPLE SAUCE BOAT
BARRY GORDON

Barry Gordon's utensils begin at the tree, usually in the form of logs, bark and all. He uses a chain saw, splitting wedges, axe, or hatchet to get the piece of wood he's selected to a manageable size. He then takes it home and coats the fresh-cut ends with wax, to allow the wood to slowly air-dry, minimizing cracking.

Next, he uses a band saw to produce the rough shape of the utensil, being careful to follow the direction in which the wood naturally grew. The exterior is then shaped using a 6" x 48" stationary belt sander, with first a coarse and then progressively finer belts. Once the outside is shaped, Gordon hollows the interior by securely clamping the workpiece and using a router with a 1¼"-diameter ball mill or similar bit. The interior surface is smoothed with sanding discs driven by a pistol-grip electric drill.

After both interior and exterior surfaces have been sanded to 220 grit, the utensils are finished by soaking in mineral oil, and sanded again by flap-wheel at 400 grit. Then a food-safe linseed oil is applied as the final finish.

MAPLE LADLES
BARRY GORDON

SCULPTURAL SPOONS
NORM SARTORIUS
(Large spoon with carved face is by Phil Payne.)

Photo by Bob Barrett

NORM SARTORIUS

Along with spoons, Norm Sartorius used to make wooden shoehorns, canes, bracelets and light switch plates, all of which he sold at craft shows in West Virginia. However, he noticed that he always got the most attention for his spoons, and he always liked making them best.

"In 1980 I did a work-study apprenticeship with a master woodworker who admired my spoons, and helped to convince me that spoons were what I should concentrate on. My aim was to do for the spoon what woodturners over the past 20 years have done for turning: they've taken it out of the everyday, and gotten people to look at it as artistic work."

As perhaps the country's leading creator of the spoon as sculptural object, Norm has clearly succeeded in reaching his goal. "There is no end to the variety this form can take. I'm crazy about rare and beautiful wood, and I get such pleasure from making something that is pleasing to the eye, pleasing to the touch, and different from anything else you've ever seen."

Norm only makes about 40 spoons a year, which are eagerly sought after by collectors, including the Smithsonian Institute in Washington, D.C., which recently purchased its first Sartorius spoon for the prestigious Renwick Gallery. He was profiled in "The Spoon As Art," a cover story in the June, 1995, edition of *Woodshop News*.

CEREMONIAL SPOONS
NORM SARTORIUS
(Ladle by Barry Gordon)

CEREMONIAL SPOONS
NORM SARTORIUS

CEREMONIAL SPOONS
NORM SARTORIUS
4 1

COLANDER, CHILI, SLOTTED & SLOW LEAKING SPOONS
WILLIAM CHAPPELOW & TOM REED

Reed left, Chappelow right

WILLIAM CHAPPELOW & TOM REED

William Chappelow and Tom Reed enjoy one of those rare artistic partnerships in which each brings out the best in the other. "Our skills have proven really complementary," Tom notes. "Bill taught me to be an artist, and I taught him how to think in business terms."

Their partnership began 20 years ago, before they knew anything about woodwork. Bill was pursuing a degree in Oceanography, and Tom worked in Hollywood negotiating recording contracts for musical groups. Neither career felt quite right, however, and at about the same time, they each found themselves headed into the mountains to try out a more pioneer-type lifestyle.

During a winter storm, a massive oak fell in the woods where Bill was living near Cuyamaca Lake in California. A few days later, Bill used a branch from that tree to stir the cauldron in which he was making natural soap. Sitting by the fire that evening, Bill found himself carving and embellishing the crude piece of oak into his first "spurtle," and as time passed, that tree proved a wellspring of spoons and stirring tools.

Bill and Tom have given their utensil enterprise the old English name of Tryyn (pronounced "treen"), literally "of the tree," which means anything made of wood used to prepare, serve or store food. Working together, Bill's creative ability and Tom's business sense provided the secure economic foundation that enabled both men to develop their love of craftsmanship. Today, their work is sold in some of the finest galleries in the country, and they have been honored by seeing their pieces purchased for the private collections of British royalty and United States presidents.

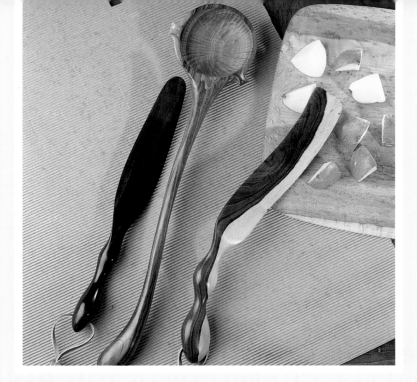

STIRRING SPURTLE, DOUBLE-SPOUTED SPOON, & SAUTEER
WILLIAM CHAPPELOW & TOM REED
(Maple Cutting Board by Ed Wohl)

SCRAMBLERS & VEGGIE PUSHERS
WILLIAM CHAPPELOW & TOM REED

SCRAMBLERS & STIR-FRYERS
WILLIAM CHAPPELOW & TOM REED

EBONY SALAD SERVERS & SALSA KNIFE
WILLIAM CHAPPELOW & TOM REED

The spoons, servers, spurtles and bowls that Bill Chappelow and Tom Reed refer to by their gallery name of "Tryyn" are all carved by hand in their California studio. The interior surfaces are oiled with mineral oil or a food-safe paraffin-based butcher's block finish. Exterior surfaces are sometimes treated with Carnauba wax and then buffed to a high sheen.

Chappelow, the master carver, has a collection of several hundred hand tools, some contemporary, and some dating back to the 1800s. Some are store-bought, and others were designed by Bill, and custom made for him by local metalsmiths.

The first step in creating one of these utensils is to rough out the shape using a gouge. It is important to attach the workpiece securely to the workbench using a clamp, vise or other sturdy holding device. The gouge is driven by a wooden hammer called a maul, the traditional round carver's tool.

Once the rough shape is formed, smaller bent-handled gouges are used, with varying degrees of "sweep," or blade curvature. Chappelow's work is distinguished by the fact that the interior surfaces are all carved, not sanded. Bill delights in creating this "fluting," the textured pattern of gouge marks, with its subtle play of shadows. Properly used, bent-handled gouges produce a surface that is actually finer and smoother than anything that could be achieved by sanding.

An abrasive technique is used in areas such as pour spouts. For these, a variety of rifflers create the rough shape of the spout, which is progressively refined and polished with files, and finally sandpaper. In 25 years of carving, Chappelow has trained himself to work with either his left or right hand, a skill he says has also kept him free from carpal tunnel syndrome, a condition that often afflicts people who perform repetitive hand motions.

IVORY-TIPPED SALAD SERVERS
LEMUEL

These servers are made from kingwood, a type of rosewood that got its name because it does not lose its color over time, a quality that led furniture makers to pronounce it the most desirable—hence the king—of all rosewoods. The blanks are band-sawed to rough shape, and the fossil walrus ivory, also rough, is glued on using epoxy. Each server is then sanded and polished on the 6" x 48" stationary belt sander, followed by vibrator sanding and oiling with mineral oil

CHARACTER SPOONS
PHIL PAYNE

SALAD FORKS & SPOONS
CHRISTINE & RON SISCO

These utensils are band-sawed from solid hardwood, then sanded to final form. For her turquoise inlay, Christine first drills a shallow, flat-bottomed hole in the handle with a Forstner bit. Using an iron mortar and pestle, she crushes turquoise rocks into a mixture of chips and dust, and using a two-part resin, fills the hole almost full with the larger chips, then tops it off with more resin, mixed with the dust. Once the resin has hardened, the inlay can be sanded just like the wood.

SPOON, KNIFE & FORK SET
HOLLY TORNHEIM

Holly has fashioned these utensils from manzanita. One-inch square blanks 9" long are band-sawed to rough shape, and then carved and sanded. The teeth of the fork are cut on the band saw, and the set is oiled with naturally polymerizing walnut oil.

SERVER SET WITH STAND
HOLLY TORNHEIM

KNIVES

DAVID BOYE KNIVES
RACHEL & MATT CONABLE

The woods used in the handles of these knives are cocobolo, redwood burl, ironwood, and cypress. The handles are cut to rough block shape, then sanded to final form. The "ring sets," as Rachel calls the detail area between handle and blade, can be made of turquoise, bone, brass, silver, or copper. The handles are sanded to 320 grit, then oiled and buffed.

RACHEL & MATT CONABLE

Rachel Conable and her husband, Matt, got their training as knife-makers in the best possible way. Rachel is the daughter of knife-maker David Boye, and she met Matt because Matt was hired to work in David's shop. Their company is now called Avalon Knives.

David Boye pioneered the Boye knife, which uses an etching process to create a raised design on the blade. Moreover, Boye knives are cast, rather than forged, which produces steel that holds an excellent edge.

Rachel began working for her father after graduating from high school. "At first I did all the little stuff any new employee gets to do, like shop cleanup, running errands, and rough grinding. I've always been interested in drawing and painting, so it wasn't long before I became involved in creating and etching the blade designs. Matt was an Economics major, and took this job originally to help pay for school."

A KNIFE TO FIT THE HAND
JOE DIGANGI

JOE DIGANGI

The sleek handles and shining steel of Joe DiGangi's chef knives seem a long way from an upstate New York dairy farm, but that was where Joe was working before he became a knife-maker. "I had always wanted to do something artistic," Joe remembers, "but pure sculpture seemed too frivolous. You can't get much more practical than a dairy farmer."

Joe had years of hands-on metalworking experience, just from making and repairing tools and equipment on the farm. "I'm an amateur gourmet chef, and I wasn't happy with the knives in my kitchen. After a while, I decided to combine the practical and the sculptural by putting an artistic form to one of the most basic shapes I knew: the knife. The concept that guided my designing was 'a knife to fit the hand.'

"One of my early knives was commissioned by a friend with arthritis. I got the shape by having her squeeze a ball of clay, which I then replicated in wood. To my surprise, I found the knife fit my hand, too. To this day, the most common reaction I get when people handle one of my knives is 'it really fits my hand!'"

The ergonomic blade shape of a DiGangi knife permits chopping with no banged knuckles. The blades themselves are surgical steel, and the handles are dyed laminated birch, infused with resin to make them waterproof and inert.

SAW-BLADE KNIFE
BRIAN CUMMINGS

The blades of these knives are made from old carpenter's saws. The handles are maple and thorn apple, selected for their gnarly and pitted appearance, and oiled with a marine-grade penetrating furniture oil.

5 6

Photo by Bob Barrett

BRIAN CUMMINGS

Brian Cummings has developed a unique way of combining wood and metal, which brings out the best qualities of both. He traces his interest in these materials to a box he found in his grandfather's barn when he was a young man.

"That box contained a bunch of antique tools. Their shapes and the way they combined wood and metal into a functional unit were fascinating, and that got me started collecting antique tools. Unfortunately, at the time I was a college student, and I didn't have the money to afford the kind of tools I coveted in antique shops, so I decided to try making my own."

Brian acquired a forge, an anvil and some metalworking tools, and began to explore tool making. "I made some kitchen utensils for myself, but I didn't like the way the bread knife cut. I looked at some of the old bread knives in my collection, and I noticed that the teeth were more sawlike than what I had made. I knew it would take me forever to cut out each sawtooth from a metal blank, so I decided to just use old saws."

Now, every weekend Brian scouts yard sales and flea markets in his native New Hampshire, buying old carpenter's saws whenever he can. He cuts the rough shape of his knife blades from the saw, then grinds and polishes them to final shape.

HAND-FORGED CARVING SET
KARL SCHROEN

The handles of this carving set are desert ironwood with a blackwood ring. The handle woods are stabilized by a special process in which they are placed in a vacuum and injected with resins, which seals the wood inside and out. With all its natural air pockets filled with resin, the wood becomes completely waterproof.

Photo by Kerry Richardson

KARL SCHROEN

Karl Schroen comes from a long line of blacksmiths. "I started out watching my grandfather at work on the forge and anvil," Karl recalls. "All the men on my father's side of the family were smiths, so it's always been in the background for me." After studying chemistry and biology in college, Karl worked as a forest entomologist, making knives only as a hobby. "I tried to fit into the American Dream, but I found the die had been cast long before: all those years spent doing other things were merely a preparation for knife making. I wouldn't have such an enjoyable life today if it weren't for the two threads of my past coming together."

Karl's chemistry and physics training gave him an advantage his forefathers might have envied: he has a keen understanding of metallurgy, and knows the chemical composition and properties of metal. This enables him to work the materials used in his tools and knife blades with extraordinary skill.

HAND-FORGED CLEAVER
KARL SCHROEN

The handle of this cleaver is made of cocobolo, with rings of blackwood and spalted alder. The woods are stabilized by a special process in which they are placed in a vacuum and injected with resins, which seals the wood inside and out. With all its natural air pockets filled with resin, the wood becomes completely waterproof.

SERVING TRAYS & CUTTING BOARDS

QUILTED CUTTING BOARD
AL LADD

The bordered quilt pattern in the cutting board shown is one of an almost infinite number of possible design variations using hardwoods crosscut to expose the end grain. As with cookies, making these cutting boards means making a batch. The design shown consists of a 13 x 13 pattern of $^3/_4$" square pieces of end-grain maple, walnut, cherry and ash, with a 2"-wide cherry and walnut border. While ripping stock to $^3/_4$" square, make trial assemblies, unglued, to explore differing patterns as you go. Use stock 10" long; after crosscutting and trimming, you should end up with about eight 1"-thick cutting boards.

QUILTED CUTTING BOARD
AL LADD

The bordered quilt pattern in this cutting board is one of an almost infinite number of possible design variations using hardwoods crosscut to expose the end grain.

As with cookies, making a cutting board like this means making a batch. Milling the 177 parts that make up the pattern is time consuming, but the best way to do it is to start out with 10"-long rails, which will later be glued up to form a 10" x 10" x 10" solid, as shown in the drawing on page 64. When crosscut, an assembly of this length will produce about eight 1"-thick finished cutting boards, or four 2"-thick boards. If you want to produce a greater number, you can begin with stock longer than 10". Do not attempt to work with stock any shorter than 10", however, as it is unsafe to rip short stock on the table saw.

The woods used in the cutting board shown are maple, cherry, ash, walnut, oak, wenge, and bloodwood. Given the natural variations in wood color, no two batches of a design like this will ever be the same. Take advantage of this opportunity for experimentation by utilizing whatever hardwoods may be available to you: even plain-looking woods may appear surprisingly good when crosscut. (In the photograph of Al Ladd's cutting board on page 62, note the interesting visual effect produced by the annual growth rings and the needle-like lines or "rays" in the oak border.)

The design shown consists of a 13 by 13 pattern of $1/2$" squares of assorted hard-woods, framed by a $1^3/4$"-wide border of oak with $1^3/4$" walnut squares at the four corners. In preparing stock for the cutting board assembly, make sure that the face of each board is flat, and that each edge makes a true right angle. To insure consistent dimensions, rip all same-sized parts in a single table saw setting.

Making an assembly with this many parts requires a clamping jig to hold the parts in place, and to distribute the clamp pressure evenly. Make this jig from four pieces of 10"-long $3/4$" plywood, one 12" wide (bottom), one $9^3/4$" wide (top), and two 11" wide (sides). Using glue and four $1^1/2$"-long wood screws, attach the edge of one of the sides to the face of the bottom to form a right angle with inside dimensions of $11^1/4$" x 11". Once the glue on this is dry, it will serve to hold the hardwood pieces in place as you build up the cutting board assembly.

To make sure you get all 177 pieces in their proper places, make a dry assembly first, outside of the jig, and then simply take it apart piece by piece as you apply glue and transfer each part to the clamping jig.

Because of the large number of surfaces requiring adhesive, it is important to use only a thin bead of glue on each face. Too much glue will turn the assembly into a sticky mess when clamp pressure is applied. Use a waterproof adhesive, one with the longest possible working time. To avoid gluing the assembly to the clamping jig, neatly line the jig with a single sheet of

QUILTED CUTTING BOARD
AL LADD

newspaper. Apply glue to the two inside faces of the lower left-hand corner block, Part A, then add two of the four oak blocks, Part B. Begin adding the $\frac{1}{2}$" blocks that form the interior pattern, completing each horizontal row before beginning the one above it.

When the last hardwood part is in place, use the remaining 11" piece of plywood to make the third side of the jig, and the $9\frac{3}{4}$" piece to make the top. Do not forget to first insert a sheet of newspaper over each face! Use a total of twenty 12" clamps, ten vertically and ten horizontally, and be sure that clamp pressure is even. Use a builder's square to check for right angles.

Once the assembly is dry, remove it from the jig and crosscut to desired thickness on the bandsaw. Surfaces may be smoothed using a thickness planer, or a hand-held 4" x 24" or similar belt sander. Finish sanding with a vibrator sander is essential, but will be time-consuming because end grain is harder than face grain.

PART	DESCRIPTION	DIMENSIONS	QUANTITY
A	Walnut Corner Block	$1\frac{3}{4}$" x $1\frac{3}{4}$" x 10"	4
B	Oak Side Block	$1\frac{3}{4}$" x $6\frac{1}{2}$" x 10"	4
C	Checkerboard Rail, Assorted Woods	$\frac{1}{2}$" x $\frac{1}{2}$" x 10"	169
D	Clamping Jig Side (Not Shown)	$\frac{3}{4}$" x 10" x 11"	2
E	Clamping Jig Bottom (Not Shown)	$\frac{3}{4}$" x 10' x 12"	1
F	Clamping Jig Top (Not Shown)	$\frac{3}{4}$" x 10" x $9\frac{3}{4}$"	1

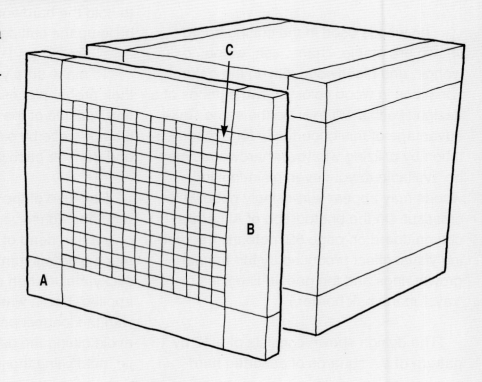

AL LADD

Al Ladd first got interested in woodworking after he landed a job in a production furniture shop. "I had always thought I'd be a teacher; unfortunately my state de-funded education while I was in college. Since I had worked as a carpenter's helper, I knew something about wood, and the furniture job showed me what incredible results you could get if you had the right machinery."

What fascinates Al most about woodworking is the way gluing together different species, with their varying grain and color combinations, can produce an infinite variety of patterns. "I have a nephew who loves turtles, and while I was at the furniture shop, I made him a turtle-shaped checker-board. That was my first introduction to edge gluing end-grain squares, and it came out so well that I began making cutting boards.

"End grain makes a lot of sense for a functional project like a cutting board: because it's so much harder than the face grain, the surface is incredibly durable. But the patterns I was creating were so beautiful that I wanted to use them more, and that led me to apply my end-grain techniques to jewelry boxes. Now I divide my time about equally between the two."

DIAMOND CUTTING BOARD
DAVE LEVY

All of the pieces shown are constructed of laminates made of walnut, maple, oak, padouk, and Finnish birch plywood. (See the directions for lamination in the General Instructions, page 11, and be sure to use a waterproof adhesive.) Dave uses a mineral-oil finish, but before applying it, he puts a coat of lacquer on the edges of the cutting boards and trays, to repel moisture.

This design starts with 24"-long laminate rods consisting of one piece of padouk, 1" thick by 1/2" wide, and three pieces of Finnish birch plywood, each 1/2" thick by 1" wide. These are edge-glued using a waterproof adhesive. After sanding and trimming to uniform size, the laminate rods are cut at a 45-degree angle to produce equilateral triangles, and then re-glued to produce the board shown.

DIAMOND CUTTING BOARD
DAVE LEVY

All of the pieces shown are constructed of laminates made of walnut, maple, oak, padouk, and Finnish birch plywood. (See the directions for lamination in the General Instructions, page 11, and be sure to use a waterproof adhesive.) Dave uses a mineral oil finish, but before applying it he puts a coat of lacquer on the edges of the cutting boards and trays to repel moisture.

The bold pattern of this laminated cutting board is an illustration of the intricate designs that can be created by gluing up laminate rods, crosscutting them at a 45-degree angle, and re-gluing them. The mirror-like effect of the pattern repetitions is enhanced by the use of Baltic Birch plywood, a commonly available commercial laminate that offers a striking visual effect at a relatively low cost. (This product has thinner laminates and fewer voids than conventional plywood.)

The design is created by making 24"-long laminate rods of 1"-wide padouk, flanked by strips of 1" and 1/2" Baltic Birch plywood. All parts are 1" thick and are assembled following the directions for lami-nations using waterproof adhesives in the General Instructions, page 11. After sanding and trimming to uniform size, the laminate rods are cut at a 45-degree angle to produce triangles, and then re-glued to produce the cutting board.

This geometric design lends itself to the individual improvisational quality that makes woodwork so interesting, as a stack of triangles offers endless recombination possibilities. Without glue, explore dry assemblies, and pick the one with the greatest visual appeal.

To glue up the pattern you eventually select, make an appropriately dimensioned clamping jig from scrap pieces of 3/4" plywood. Use single sheets of newspaper to avoid gluing the cutting board to the clamping jig. Use waterproof adhesive, and make sure clamp pressure is evenly distributed. When the assembly is dry, a thickness planer or hand-held 4" x 24" belt sander can be used to smooth the face of your cutting board, followed by vibrator sanding, and a coat of mineral oil.

VALENTINE SERVING TRAY
DAVE LEVY

Edge glue 1" x 1" x 12" pieces of walnut, maple, padouk and oak using waterproof adhesive. The heart shape is cut out on a band saw, and a router is used to remove the material in the center of the tray. After sanding, the edges of the tray are sprayed with lacquer to repel moisture. When this is dry, the remainder of the tray is oiled with mineral oil.

Photo by Bob Barrett

ED WOHL

Ed Wohl has always been interested in woodwork, but the seeds for his cutting boards were planted when he was studying to be an architect. "I had the good fortune to work with an industrial designer, and that experience got me interested in making the kind of scale models architects sometimes use to show what a building project will look like. After a while, I found I enjoyed spending the day in the model-making shop much more than I enjoyed spending the day in the office."

Ed's interest led him to begin to design and build his own furniture. "I had begun exhibiting my work at local art fairs, and I found it was nice to have a low-priced item people could buy when they couldn't make up their minds to buy a table or desk ." Cutting boards were the perfect solution.

There was another reason why cutting boards fit so well into Ed's workshop. "When I hired a helper, the first thing I trained him to do was make cutting boards. They require you to use just about every tool in the shop, and once you've mastered them, you're ready to work on furniture."

Ed was encouraged to expand his production by Robert Schaps, owner of Citywoods Gallery in Highland Park, Illinois, a longtime admirer of Ed's work. By using computer-operated machinery, Ed was able to lower his production costs, thus making the boards affordable for more people, while still maintaining their quality and unique appeal.

BIRDSEYE MAPLE CUTTING BOARD
ED WOHL

This ³/₄"-thick cutting board is made of birdseye maple. Three pieces of wood are edge-glued with a waterproof glue, then band-sawed to rough shape. The edges of the board are curved using a 6" x 48" stationary belt sander, and then vibrator-sanded, and the handle hole is drilled on the drill press. After sanding, the board is twice dipped in water to raise the grain, allowed to dry, and then sanded again after each wetting. Finally, it is dipped in mineral oil. This wetting-and-sanding process means that in actual use, the board keeps its smooth surface even after getting wet.

BIRDSEYE MAPLE CUTTING BOARD
ED WOHL

This beautiful and highly serviceable cutting board is a straightforward laminate of three pieces of $\frac{1}{2}$"-thick birdseye maple, edge-glued using waterproof glue, then bandsawed to rough shape. The edges of the board are curved and given a rounded profile using a 6" x 48" stationary belt sander and hand files, and then vibrator sanded. The handle hole is drilled on the drill press.

As the cutting board takes shape, it becomes an object of increasing beauty. Like all cutting boards, however, its fate is to be subjected to the worst conditions any piece of fine woodwork can suffer: frequent contact with water, and the ravages of the knife. In order to keep it looking good for as long as possible, Ed Wohl has developed a special technique.

After the first finish sanding, and before oiling, Ed briefly dips the entire cutting board in water. This causes the exterior wood cells to swell, and produces an effect that is called "raising the grain." (In another context, this technique can be used to remove small dents and dings in wood furniture.) After it dries, the cutting board now has a rough, furry feel, so Ed subjects it to a second vibrator sanding. This water-dip/let dry/finish sand procedure is then repeated a second time, and only afterward is the cutting board given its mineral oil finish.

As a result, the appearance of Ed Wohl's cutting boards does not change dramatically upon contact with water. By using Eastern hard rock maple, Ed insures that this cutting board will keep its good looks through years of service, despite the effects of knives like those made by Joe DiGangi (page 54) and Brian Cummings (page 56).

PART	DESCRIPTION	DIMENSIONS	QUANTITY
A	Handle Section	$\frac{1}{2}$" x 3" x 15$\frac{1}{2}$"	1
B	Side Section	$\frac{1}{2}$" x 2$\frac{1}{2}$" x 9$\frac{1}{2}$"	2

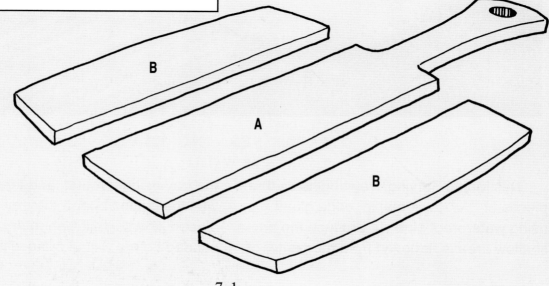

MAPLE SERVING TRAY
ED WOHL

This Maple Serving Tray begins as three pieces of $^{13}/_{16}$"-thick maple, edge glued using waterproof glue. To produce the rim, a shallow area is removed from the center of the tray using a router, and then sanded. As with the cutting board, the tray is twice-dipped in water, allowed to dry, and then re-sanded before a final oiling with mineral oil.

RIBBED TRAY
HOLLY TORNHEIM

This serving tray is made from Mozambican panga-panga wood, a species that has recently come on the market thanks to a sustainable yield forestry project. The tray begins as a piece of 2"-thick wood, and as with all her pieces, Holly removes the excess with carvers' gouges and by sanding. The finished piece is oiled with naturally polymerizing walnut oil.

KOA SERVING PLATTER
MARC GARDNER

Marc uses a chain saw to shape the rough form of this platter, which is based on an ancient Hawaiian original in the Bishop Museum in Honolulu. All the carving is done by hand with chisels and gouges. The finished form is sanded by hand and with a vibrator sander. Marc uses a vegetable-based penetrating oil finish.

Photo by Nancy Gardner

MARC GARDNER

Marc Gardner's woodwork is dedicated to the Hawaiian tradition of kalua, or underground oven cooking. Following the ancient ways, kalua begins with the imu, a deep pit dug in the earth, then filled with firewood and covered with hundreds of fist-sized lava beach rocks. Wrapped in banana or ti leaves, foods such as yams, potatoes, turkey or pork go on top, covered by more leaves, until they are steamed to perfection.

Eager diners are served the products of this marvellous slow cooker on Marc's platters, hand carved from native Hawaiian woods such as koa, milo, or ohia. His teacher, a German emigrant named William Hopfe who arrived in the islands in the late 1800s, learned about kalua and the imu from the full-blooded Hawaiian woman who later became his wife.

"Growing up in a small town outside Honolulu, I knew about the luau and Hawaiian food customs," Marc observes. "I met William Hopfe when I moved to the big island, and when he offered to teach me how to make his kalua boards, I jumped at the chance. He taught me the importance of complementing the food.

"My boards are meant to create the airspace around what's being served. What I do allows the food to be held in a lifted, exalted position. Starting with a solid block of wood, I use gouges and chisels to carve out the final shape. The wood that was there is what makes the wood that is there ethereal, airborne".

BOCOTE CUTTING BOARD
TONY LYDGATE

Hardwood logs of many species often include lighter colored areas of sapwood, the portion of the tree just under the bark. In bocote, a hardwood grown in Northern Mexico, the contrast between the sapwood and the darker heartwood can be quite dramatic, a feature Tony's cutting board takes advantage of. A 5"-wide board is ripped into three pieces, preserving the natural heartwood-sapwood pattern. Thin rippings of rosewood, purpleheart and osage orange are glued in between the bocote, using waterproof adhesive, and the finished board is oiled with mineral oil.

A TOUCH OF
THE EAST

EBONY AND MAPLE CHOPSTICKS & TRAY
TOM DAVIN & MARY KESSLER

The elegant tray is made of maple and ebony. The inset in the center of the tray is a piece of $3/4$"-thick figured maple, which is suspended inside the ebony frame. Two $1/2$"-square maple rails, dadoed into the underside of the maple block, fit into slots on the insides of the long sides of the frame. The short sides of the frame are given a slight curve by band sawing and sanding wider stock.

The maple accents on the ends of the chopsticks can produce either a straight line or a chevron design, depending on how the chopsticks are placed together. Tom and Mary prepare a laminate rod of alternating $1/16$" strips of maple and ebony, using water-proof glue. This rod is then sliced at a 45-degree angle, and the accent pieces glued to the ends of the chopstick blanks, which are hand-sanded to final shape and oiled with mineral oil.

EBONY AND MAPLE CHOPSTICKS & TRAY
TOM DAVIN & MARY KESSLER

This maple and ebony tray and chopsticks set shows how a simple design, skillfully executed in fine materials, can produce a sophisticated effect.

The maple surface of the tray is a single piece of $3/4$"-thick Eastern hard maple, slightly rounded on the corners and edges, suspended inside an ebony frame with four $1/4$" dowels.

Tom and Mary have deliberately selected a piece of maple with personality. Note the irregular grain pattern produced by the wood's annual growth rings, as well as the cluster of birdseyes, and the two mineral streaks. Although naturally occurring irregularities like these appear to some observers as defects, to Tom and Mary they are the expressions of uniqueness that give a piece of wood, like a person, its distinctive character.

Use a $1/4$" drill bit to bore four $1/4$" deep holes in the edges of Part A, the maple center. Using the 6" x 48" belt sander or a handheld file, slightly round the circular edges of the ends of the four dowels, Part B. (This makes it easier to insert them.) Apply a small amount of glue to each hole in Part A and tap in the dowels. Mark the location of the dowel holes on the inside face of the sides, Part C, and then drill them, being careful not to allow the drill to penetrate any deeper than $1/8$".

Use a $1/4$"-wide dado blade to mill the dados in the handles and sides, and drill from underneath for the pins that hold the handles in place. Drill through the dado and into the upper portion of the side so that the pin can extend approximately $1/8$" past the dado. Select a drill bit very slightly smaller in diameter than the brass pin, so that it will create a tight "jam fit" when installed. (In a pinch, you can always sand the pin down to appropriate diameter.)

If you have a 6" x 48" belt sander with an exposed drive or idler cylinder, use it to give the handles a slight curve on their outer edge. (If this tool is unavailable, use the bandsaw, followed by filing and sanding.) After all parts have been finish sanded, assemble with a small amount of waterproof glue in the dado and on the tips of the dowels.

The chopsticks start out as ebony blanks, each $5/16$" x $5/16$" x $9 1/2$". To create the chevron detail on opposing faces at their square ends, Tom uses a thin-kerf saw blade to make $1/16$"-deep slots, either straight across the grain, or at a 45-degree angle. These are filled with glued-in $1/16$" strips of maple that have been milled on the table saw. The assembly looks messy while it is underway, but once the glue is dried and the excess sanded off, the result is as shown.

The chopsticks maintain their square shape throughout the length of the taper, so they can be made on the belt sander. The solid ebony chopstick rests are given a curved profile, and drilled so that each will accommodate one pair of chopsticks.

PART	DESCRIPTION	DIMENSIONS	QUANTITY
A	Tray Center	$3/4$" x 7" x 14"	1
B	Dowels	$1/4$" x $5/8$"	4
C	Sides	$3/8$" x 1" x 16"	2
D	Handles	$1/4$" x 1" x 9"	2
E	Brass Pin	$1/16$" x $3/4$"	4

PART	DESCRIPTION	DIMENSIONS	QUANTITY
F	Chopstick Blank (Not Drawn)	$5/16$" x $5/16$" x $9 1/2$"	2
G	Maple Chevron (Not Drawn)	$1/16$" x $1/16$" x 10"	1
H	Chopstick Rest (Not Drawn)	$1 1/2$" x $3/4$" x $3/4$"	2

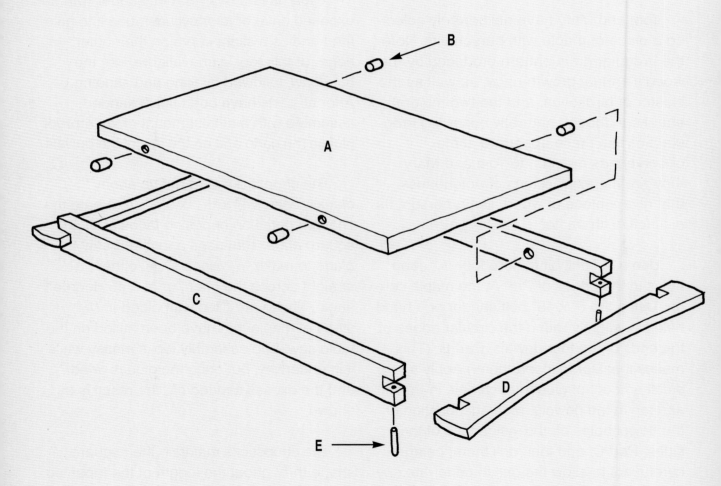

Photo by Bob Barrett

TOM DAVIN & MARY KESSLER

Tom Davin and Mary Kessler met in a college art class. "Tom was always working in the wood-shop, so if I wanted to see him, that's where I'd go," says Mary. "I'm not the kind of person who could sit there and do nothing, so I began to help out. One thing led to another, and it wasn't long before our woodwork was helping to put both of us through college."

Tom and Mary's success comes from their ability to combine creative design with skilful production. A visit to their booth at a craft fair reveals an eye-catching assortment of highly functional objects, from trays and chopsticks to letter openers and boxes. Each reflects the bold but graceful shapes that have become their trademark.

"Tom is the main designer and the powerhouse in the shop," Mary notes at their Rhode Island studio. "He's particularly good at making the jigs and templates we need to produce multiples. Now that we have three kids, I've been spending less time in the shop and more time making sure we're running things in a businesslike way."

CHOPSTICKS
HOLLY TORNHEIM

These chopsticks and the rests they sit on are made from manzanita. After making blanks ¹/₂" square by 12" long, Holly uses a Dremel-type handheld sander to carve the desired shape.

LEMUEL

"My dad had tools and a workbench, and the first woodworking project I can remember as a kid was making swords. I kept at it, taking shop classes in high school and reading all the woodworking books I could find. I do a lot of cabinet work now, but I still love making the kind of handheld objects you actually use in your everyday life."

Lemuel began exhibiting his serving utensils, chopsticks and trays at craft fairs, and was invited in 1983 to join the prestigious Northwest Gallery of Fine Woodworking in Seattle, where his work is shown today. "Two things I'm interested in, bonsai and sea mammals, are the biggest influences on my woodworking. With bonsai, the naturally curved forms of these miniature trees just kind of grow in their own organic way. That led me to use the natural edge you see on the Maple Burl Serving Trays (page 78). Animals like seals, porpoises and orcas have such streamlined shapes, and that's what I was thinking about when I developed the ergonomic shapes of my chopsticks and servers."

Lemuel tips these servers and chopsticks with fossil walrus ivory. "I only use the fossilized material, which is mined by native Alaskans from traditional fishing sites that have been used by man for tens of thousands of years."

MAPLE BURL SERVING TRAY
LEMUEL

Lemuel selects a slab of inch-thick western broadleaf maple burl with the exterior edge, bark removed, still in place. A router with a dovetail bit is used to make the slots for the rosewood feet, which are similarly shaped and glued in with epoxy or waterproof glue. The finished piece is oiled with mineral oil.

KINGWOOD CHOPSTICKS
LEMUEL

A piece of fossilized walrus ivory, $1/2$" square by $1/4$" thick, is glued on the end of a $1/2$"-square kingwood blank, $9^1/2$" long, using epoxy. When dry, each chopstick is shaped on the 6" x 48" belt sander, then hand-sanded and oiled with mineral oil.

CHOPSTICKS IN SILK PANTS
TONY LYDGATE

These chopsticks begin as $5/16$"-square blanks, each $9\frac{1}{2}$" long. They are loaded into the chuck of a pistol-grip drill, and rotated while being pressed onto a moving 6" x 48" belt sander with a 120x belt. The angle at which the sticks are held is just high enough off the horizontal to produce the appropriate taper. After the tapered half of the stick is shaped, the square shank is flat-sanded on the same machine. The end of the shank is given a slight four-point bevel, and the stick is oiled in mineral oil. The cases are stitched from silk.

Photo by Judy Dater

TONY LYDGATE

For woodworker, author and educator Tony Lydgate, cutting boards came about as a by-product of another woodworking project. "I had been making elaborate backgammon sets, with the playing surfaces cut from exotic wood veneers, and I used solid Hawaiian koa for the case parts. This left me with some leftover koa rippings, and it occurred to me that I could laminate them with contrasting woods."

The cutting boards looked so great that Tony took them to a local craft fair. "This was the first time I had ever tried to sell my woodwork to the general public. I had that marvellous shock that so many woodworkers experience on their first sale: you mean people will actually pay me money to do what I love?"

Although Tony has expanded his utensil designs to include chopsticks and a sushi set, he is probably best known for his boxes. As the author of *The Art of Making Elegant Wood Boxes* and *Award Winning Wood Boxes: Design and Technique*, both published by Chapelle/Sterling, he has brought the work of dozens of the country's leading box-makers to a wide public audience. Also, Tony's articles on woodworking and the vital role of crafts have appeared in leading national publications.

"Our nation has a proud tradition of the importance of the handmade. As we're increasingly swamped with poorly made mass-produced goods, more and more people are seeking out America's fine handcrafters. I'm honored to count myself a member of this marvellous group of creative individuals, and I'm dedicated to doing everything I can to spread the good word about their work."

Tony Lydgate is a leading advocate for fine American handcrafts and is a Trustee of the American Craft Council.

SUSHI SET FOR TWO
TONY LYDGATE

Sushi is a dish of morsels of seasoned rice filled or topped with fresh vegetables or seafood. To make this sushi tray, a 5$\frac{1}{2}$"-wide piece of $\frac{3}{4}$"-thick birdseye maple is ripped into five 1"-wide pieces, each 13" long. A table saw with dado blade is used to mill a $\frac{1}{8}$"-deep slot $\frac{1}{2}$" in from the end of the pieces, just wide enough to hold two pairs of chopsticks. A similar slot is milled on the other end of the three central pieces. This slot will hold the two-compartment rosewood dish, used for the two condiments traditionally eaten with sushi: a green horseradish

called wasabi, and gari, or pickled ginger. The tray stands on and is held together by two 1"-wide by $\frac{1}{2}$"-thick rosewood feet, glued with waterproof adhesive into a $\frac{3}{8}$"-deep dado milled on the underside of the tray. The dado and the bottoms of the feet are angled 32 degrees. The compartments on the 2" x 4" x $\frac{1}{2}$" rosewood mixing dish are milled using a router. All parts are rounded and sanded, and the resulting tray is oiled with mineral oil. Chopsticks are made as described on page 80 from maple and rosewood.

SUSHI SET FOR TWO
TONY LYDGATE

Sushi is a dish of morsels of seasoned rice filled or topped with fresh vegetables or seafood. To make this sushi tray, start with a $5\frac{1}{2}$"-wide piece of $\frac{3}{4}$"-thick birdseye maple. Use an abrasive planer to flatten and smooth both faces of the maple blank, and crosscut it to exactly 13" in length, being careful to ensure that all the corners are right angles. Rip the blank into five 1"-wide pieces. (Throughout the assembly process, keep the pieces in the order in which they were ripped, to preserve the original grain pattern.)

Next, a dado blade is used to mill dados for the feet, the chopsticks, and the mixing dish. For the feet, use a $\frac{1}{2}$" dado, angled 32 degrees from the vertical. Move the table saw fence to the left of the blade, and set it so that the dado cut starts $1\frac{1}{2}$" in from the end of the maple slats. Adjust blade height so that the shallowest point of the angled cut is about $\frac{1}{8}$". Use the miter gauge, set at 90 degrees, in passing the slats over the blade. Solid backing on the miter gauge will prevent tear-out at the end of the cut.

For the slot into which the two pairs of chopsticks will be set, return the dado blade to true vertical, and increase its width to $\frac{5}{8}$". With the table saw fence in its usual position to the right of the blade, mill the slot $1\frac{1}{4}$" wide by making two $\frac{1}{8}$"-deep passes, beginning $\frac{1}{2}$" in from the end of the stock.

Two condiments are traditionally eaten with sushi: wasabi, a spicy green horserad-ish that is often mixed with soy sauce, and gari, or pickled ginger, and this sushi set includes a two-compartment rosewood dish to hold them. The dish sits in a slot $\frac{1}{8}$" deep, like the one that holds the chopsticks, but this slot is milled in only the central three of the sushi board's five slats, so set the outer two slats temporarily aside. Like the chopsticks slot, it starts at $\frac{1}{2}$" in from the end, but since it is $1\frac{7}{8}$" wide, three passes of the dado blade will be needed to mill it.

The tray stands on and is held together by two 1" x 6" rosewood feet, each $\frac{1}{2}$" thick, glued with waterproof adhesive into the dado milled on the underside of the tray. The lower face of each foot is angled at 32 degrees. Start with 1" x 1" x $\frac{1}{2}$" stock, then angle the table saw blade to 32 degrees, move the fence to the left of the blade, and rip.

Prior to assembly, use the 6" x 48" belt sander to sand the top and bottom faces of each maple slat, and give the long edges of the top surface an eased radius or slight rounding. To glue, turn the entire assembly upside down on the workbench, and use four 8"-long pieces of scrap $\frac{1}{4}$" plywood to maintain the correct distance between the five slats. The ends of the feet should extend slightly beyond the edges of the outer slats.

After the glue is dry, use the 6" x 48" sander to sand off this excess, to smooth the sides and ends of the sushi board, and to give all edges the same slight rounding. The

SUSHI SET FOR TWO
TONY LYDGATE

board is now ready to oil with mineral oil.

The mixing dish itself is a rosewood blank $1/2$" x $1^7/_8$" x 4". The two shallow compartments are milled with a router. Chopsticks are made from maple and rosewood as described on page 86.

PART	DESCRIPTION	DIMENSIONS	QUANTITY
A	MapleSlat	$3/_4$" x 1" x 13"	5
B	Foot	$1/_2$" x 1" x 6"	2
C	Mixing Dish	$1/_2$" x $1^7/_8$" x 4"	1
D	Chopsticks (Not Drawn)	$5/_{16}$" x $5/_{16}$" x $9^1/_2$"	2

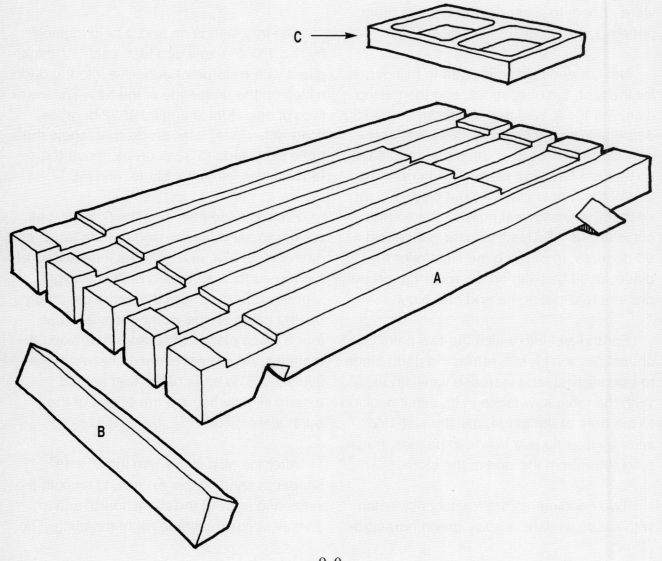

FOR THE REST OF
THE KITCHEN

CHEESE MOUSE
BRAD SMITH
(Cutting Board by Ed Wohl)

This cheese slicer is as amusingly shaped as it is effective. The cutting edge is a section of fisherman's leader wire, held in place and tightened by a stock threaded brass knob.

Photo by Bob Barrett

BRAD SMITH

Brad Smith's interest in woodworking started in high school and followed him to the Rochester Institute of Technology School for American Craftsmen, where he studied furniture design. As part of his course of study, he designed a series of utensils, including the tongs and trivets shown on pages 86 and 87.

In 1980, Brad set up shop on his father's Pennsylvania farm, and began producing some of his original design school projects on a larger scale. "At that time, making furniture seemed a little out of my reach: my shop was too small, and I didn't have the capital for the machinery I needed. The success of the utensils has enabled me to get better equipped, and now furniture is my main interest."

The farm-life surroundings have become incorporated into Brad's woodwork. Items as unlikely as pitchforks, axe handles, tractor seats and disc blades have all appeared as elements in his furniture.

Brad owns an unusual piece of machinery called an axe-handle lathe, which is about a hundred years old. He uses it to make furniture legs and lamp and bed posts. The machine creates an interesting surface texture, which Brad emphasizes by painting and then sanding through the paint.

RUBBER BAND TONGS
BRAD SMITH

Brad uses close-grained woods like maple and cherry for his tongs. Blanks are band-sawn from 2"-thick stock into their S-curve shape, but left about $1/2$" thick, then band-sawed again into two pieces, which make the two halves of the tongs when one is flipped over. The band-sawed surfaces are smoothed on a pneumatic drum sander, and a notch is cut to hold the "rubber band"— actually a short section of long-lasting latex tubing.

LEATHER-FOOTED
NAPKIN HOLDER
BRAD SMITH

In this ingenious design, a small piece of leather, glued into a dado on the inside face of each of the two wood blocks, forms the bottom of the napkin holder, holding its two pieces together. The blocks themselves are band-sawed and sanded from cherry or any available wood. Their end-grain bases are cut at a slight angle from the horizontal, so that each is slightly "standing on its toes." Because each block wants to tip inward, they provide just the right amount of pressure to hold the napkins neatly in place.

NUTCRACKER
BRAD SMITH

The wooden parts of this nutcracker are made from maple, cherry or oak, rough cut on a band saw and then sanded to shape. Brad has the jaws custom-cast from bronze; as an alternative, try modifying a metal hinge, or insetting two sections of a coarse file.

CRISS-CROSS TRIVET
BRAD SMITH

CRISS-CROSS TRIVET
BRAD SMITH

In this trivet design, shown here in red oak, notches are cut halfway through $1/2$"-square lengths of hardwood in such a way that the lengths can be fitted together. Many variations of this simple concept are possible, but they all have one crucial element in common: the assembly will not work unless the spacing of the notches is exact.

Since the table saw is the most commonly available tool, here is a technique for using a table saw with a dado blade to create exact spacing in rail notches. First, the dado blade should be carbide tipped, and sharp. Second, the width of the notch must be the same as the thickness of the stock being used. If you use a dado blade set to make a $1/2$" notch, then the finished thickness of the stock must be $1/2$".

Prepare stock, including finish sanding, at least on the thickness dimension, prior to making the notch. The design calls for eight rails, but it's not much more difficult to make 16 or even 32, so consider making the trivets in a batch. In addition, make several extra rails, either from hardwood or scrap, to use as test pieces.

Make sure that the rails are identical in length, exactly 12", and that both butts are cleanly crosscut. The first notch begins at $3^1/2$" in from the end of the rail, so use the measuring guide on the table saw to set the fence at precisely $3^1/2$". With the miter gauge set to exactly 90 degrees, notch test pieces until two of them fit together exactly,

which should occur when the depth of cut is exactly half the height of the rail. Make sure the miter gauge has a backing of solid material, to prevent tear-out as the dado blade passes through the stock.

Now you are ready to mill the first notch in your stock. You can mill at least eight pieces per pass over the dado blade: make sure the stock is both flat on the saw table and tight against the fence, and do not allow fingers to come near the moving blade.

In the design shown, the three spaces between the four rails are squares exactly 1" on a side, so the location for the second notch is established by setting the table saw fence at precisely 5": $1/2$" for the thickness of the first notch, plus 1" to separate it from the second. When milling the second and all other notches, be sure that the same end of the stock is against the fence at each pass over the dado blade.

Adding $1^1/2$" to the fence measurement each time produces settings of $6^1/2$" for the third notch, and 8" for the fourth notch. Since the overall length of the stock is 12", the first notch should start at an identical $3^1/2$" in from either end. If it does not, do not worry—as long as you started from the same end for each cut, the trivet will still assemble, and if one set of ends is more (or less) than $3^1/2$", you can simply trim off the excess. Bevel the ends slightly on the 6" x 48" stationery belt sander, glue with waterproof glue, and oil with mineral oil.

CRISS-CROSS TRIVET
BRAD SMITH

An alternative technique is to use the same tools to mill four notches or dados across a 12"-long piece of $1/2$"-thick hardwood, about $5^1/2$" wide, and then rip it into $1/2$"-thick strips after the dados have been cut. The strips must be ripped slightly thicker than $1/2$", and then sanded on both sides until they are the right size to fit the notches.

PART	DESCRIPTION	DIMENSIONS	QUANTITY
A	Notched Trivet Rail	$1/2$" x $1/2$" x 12"	8

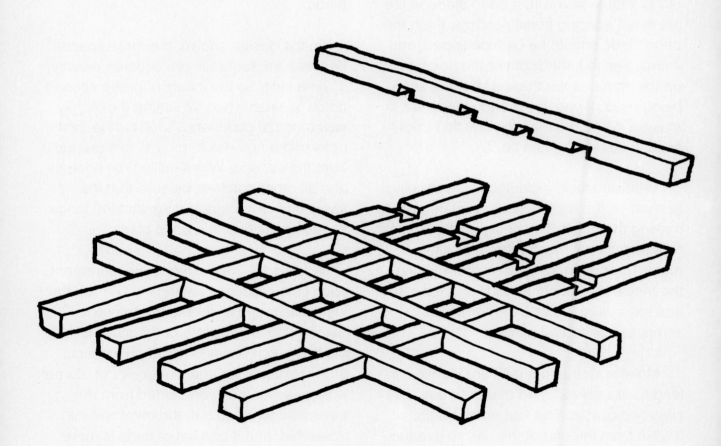

WISHBONE SPOON, COFFEE MEASURE & OLIVE THIEF
WILLIAM CHAPPELOW & TOM REED

PASTA SET
WILLIAM CHAPPELOW & TOM REED

CHRISTINE & RON SISCO

Christine Sisco has a degree in business, and she's only a utensil maker part-time, but she's quick to note that woodwork is her favorite activity. "At this time in my life, my woodwork is the most gratifying thing I do. It's my passion, and when I get involved in it, everything else can go by the wayside."

Eight years ago, Christine was managing a family business when she asked her engineer husband to show her how to make the bread knives he'd been producing as a hobby. "Since I've always loved to cook, particularly gourmet-style Northern Italian and Mexican dishes, making kitchen utensils was a natural for me. Once I got started on the bread knives, I began to branch out to spoons and forks, spatulas, rolling pins and servers."

Treestump Woodworks, as Christine and Ron call their business, has grown steadily since then. "I test everything in my own kitchen before we start producing it for our customers. That's where a number of our designs originated: I'd realize I wanted a certain kitchen tool I didn't have, so I'd go out and make it myself. My mother always told me I could do anything I wanted in life, and today, what I enjoy most is creating good designs that are really functional, that people can use everyday."

ROLLING PIN
CHRISTINE & RON SISCO

These rolling pins are lathe-turned from a laminated wood product called Colorwood, produced by the Rutland Plywood Company of Rutland, Vermont.

BREADBOARD
& BREAD KNIFE
CHRISTINE & RON SISCO

This traditional bread knife design is given a contemporary look by using Colorwood. The basic form of the bread knife is cut out on a band saw, and the edges are then rounded by sanding.

Photo by Bob Barrett

DAVE LEVY

"I like making things work, and figuring out how to do something," says Dave Levy, whose laminated cutting boards, trays, napkin holders, rolling pins, and salt and pepper shakers are a familiar sight at craft exhibitions. "I started out wanting to be an architect, but when I went to design school, I got interested in woodwork."

Dave says that after finishing school, he "plunged right into the art show circuit," creating a market for his designs that would provide him with the means to develop and refine them. In addition to the pieces shown here, Dave's studio near Davis, California, also makes wood game sets, including dominoes, backgammon, checkers, and cribbage. His most impressive piece is a modular game table, with a reversible top for either chess/checkers or backgammon.

"Trying to make things that are impossible to make is the greatest challenge for me. That's what I like about wood. With so many problems to deal with—finding the right species, maintaining proper moisture content, meeting demands for special machinery and tooling—of all the media, wood presents the greatest challenge."

FINGER-JOINTED NAPKIN HOLDER DAVE LEVY

Dave Levy's signature laminate technique is used to produce this simple but ingenious napkin holder. Edge-glue $3/4$"-thick strips of walnut, maple, oak and padouk to 8" width and 16" length, then crosscut to produce two 6"-long sides and one 4"-long base. A router with jig is used to mill finger joints in both end-grain ends of each piece. The base and one end of each side are drilled to receive the pin that holds the sides to the base and allows them to swivel.

LAMINATED SALT & PEPPER SHAKERS DAVE LEVY

A laminate is made from a 1" x 3" x 24" piece of walnut, flanked symmetrically by thinner strips of maple and padouk, and finally by 1" x 3" x 24" pieces of oak. The resulting laminate rod is crosscut into 4" lengths, each of which will become one shaker. A drill press makes a cavity in the bottom, secured by a rubber stopper, to hold the contents, along with the small dispenser holes in the top. The shaker is then shaped on a belt sander and given a lacquer finish.

COASTERS
DAVE LEVY
1 0 5

COASTERS
DAVE LEVY

This six-piece coaster set in walnut, oak, maple, and padouk comes with its own storage cup. The six 4"-square coasters are crosscut from a 25" laminate. In milling lumber for this laminate, be sure each piece of stock starts with a flat face, so that its edges will be straight, and form a true right angle. For assembly, follow the directions for laminations using waterproof adhesives in the General Instructions, page 11.

Once the laminate is dry, trim the butts and crosscut into six 4" lengths. The shallow circular depression that holds the cork liner is made with a router. (For a complete guide to routers and how to use them, consult your local bookstore or library for books on router technique published by Sterling.)

Unlike most woodwork, a coaster's sole purpose in life is to come in contact with water, and this demands appropriate precautions. The lamination must be glued up with a waterproof adhesive, and a water resistant finish should be used. After the coasters have been shaped and sanded, and their edges and corners rounded, apply at least two coats of lacquer or varnish. Sand between coats, and follow manufacturer's instructions, both for proper application of the finish, and for safe working conditions during use.

Sheet cork in various thicknesses may be obtained from hobby shops or specialty catalogs. At the final step, use waterproof adhesive to attach the circular cork liner.

The cup that holds the coasters is made following the same laminate techniques as the coasters themselves. Although it is not technically essential to use waterproof adhesive for the cup, there is something to be said for using comparable materials in all phases of a project. Because of the difficulty of ripping short pieces of wood on the table saw, two cups at a time should be made, which is why cup parts are listed as 12" in length, instead of the finish length of 6".

A router is used to create the interior space of the cup. Exterior surfaces are sanded and rounded, and the cup is given the same finish as the coasters.

PART	DESCRIPTION	DIMENSIONS	QUANTITY
A	Maple Laminate	$1/2"$ x $3/4"$ x 25"	2
B	Walnut Laminate	$1/2"$ x $7/8"$ x 25"	2
C	Maple Laminate	$1/2"$ x $1/8"$ x 25"	2
D	Padouk Laminate	$1/2"$ x 1'2" x 25"	1
E	Cork Liner	$3 1/2"$ diameter x $1/8"$	6
F	Oak Cup Laminates (Not Drawn; Stock to Make Two Cups)	$3/4"$ x $1 3/4"$ x 12"	2
	Walnut	$3/4"$ x $1 3/4"$ x 12"	2
	Maple	$1/2"$ x $1 3/4"$ x 12"	1
	Maple	$1/8"$ x $1 3/4"$ x 12"	2
	Padouk	$1/4"$ x $1 3/4"$ x 12"	2

Because coasters are designed for use with water, make sure the laminates and the cork liner are glued using a waterproof adhesive.

The wooden portions of the coaster should be treated with a marine-grade varnish.

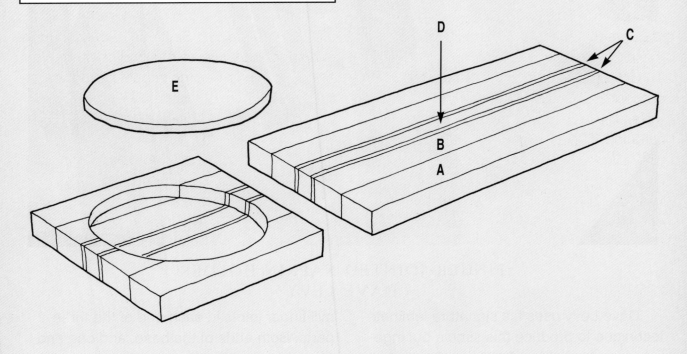

FINGER-JOINTED NAPKIN HOLDER
DAVE LEVY

Dave Levy uses his signature laminate technique to produce this simple but ingenious napkin holder. A 17"-long laminate is formed by edge gluing ³/₄"-thick strips of walnut, maple, oak, and padouk, which is crosscut to produce two 6"-long sides and one 4"-long base. A router jig is then used to mill finger joints in each end of the three parts. Both ends of the base, and one end of each side, are drilled to receive the wooden dowel that holds the sides to the base and allows them to swivel. All parts are shaped, rounded, sanded, and then given a lacquer finish.

PART	DESCRIPTION	DIMENSIONS	QUANTITY
A	Walnut Laminate	$3/4$" x $1 3/4$" x 17"	2
B	Oak Laminate	$3/4$" x $1 3/4$" x 17"	2
C	Walnut Laminate	$1/2$" x $3/4$" x 17"	2
D	Maple Laminate	$1/16$" x $3/4$" x 17"	2
E	Padouk Laminate	$1/2$" x $3/4$" x 17"	1
F	Hinge Dowel	$1/8$" diameter x $8 5/8$"	2

The woods used in the photo on page 108 are walnut, maple, oak, and padouk. Any combination of available woods may be used in making this napkin holder. It is especially adaptable for using home-grown, or locally available woods that can be harvested by the woodworker.

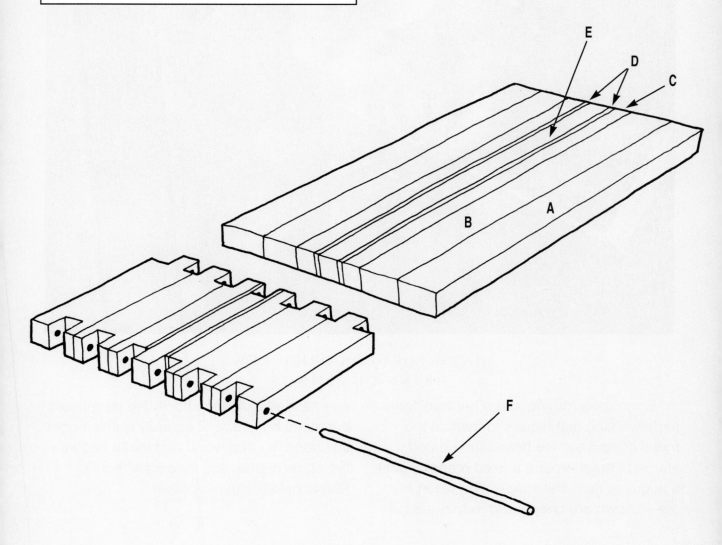

HAND-FORGED CORKSCREW
BRIAN CUMMINGS

Brian uses forging and other traditional metalworking techniques to fashion the metal corkscrew. He bends the heated stainless steel around a fixed mandrel until it acquires its spiral shape. The wood handle—shown are cherry and maple—is cut and sanded to rough shape. He then heats the metal handle, and actually burns it onto the wood, so that wood and metal become the same shape, assuring a perfect fit. Rivets hold the two together.

TRADITIONAL PEPPER & SALT MILL
DEBORAH DOYLE

For those who prefer their pepper freshly ground, this traditional turned rosewood design is ideal. Available through craft cata- logs, the metal grinding mechanism is used in the salt version as well.

ROSEWOOD SERVING TONGS
DEBORAH DOYLE

These tongs are cut out on a band saw, then shaped on a 6" x 48" belt sander using progressively finer grits. The ends are glued together with waterproof glue. It is important that the arms of the tongs be thin enough to be flexible. Tongs are oiled with mineral oil or other food-safe finish.

OVAL SALT & PEPPER SHAKERS
DEBORAH DOYLE

Each shaker is turned on a lathe, then given a flat bottom by sawing off a section. Holes for the salt and pepper are drilled using a $1/16$"-diameter drill bit. The refilling hole in the base is $3/8$" diameter, and is kept plugged with a small cork. Shakers are oiled with hand-rubbed Danish-oil finish.

DEBORAH DOYLE

Deborah Doyle specializes in creating rosewood utensils that offer the perfect marriage between the functional and the artistic. Her most sought-after pieces are made from a species of rosewood called cocobolo (Dahlbergia retusa), prized for its dense, almost metallic hardness, and its deep, rich color.

"I was trained as a biochemist, but after a 15-year career, the day came when I realized I couldn't stand being locked up in a lab any longer. I took a long vacation to sort out what I wanted to do next. My trip didn't yield any immediate answers, but in one of the countries I visited, I did discover cocobolo, and I brought some back with me."

It wasn't long before Deborah tried turning some of her wood on a lathe, part of a well-equipped workshop owned by friends who had a business repairing farm machinery. "Rosewood polishes and finishes so beautifully, and the lathe is such a versatile tool. I started out making bracelets, which I sold at craft fairs. Then I got a large order for bracelets from a department store, and that enabled me to buy my own equipment, and to perfect my technique through study with master turners."

Deborah sees a close parallel between her two careers. "Good science and good art are alike," she observes. "Both strive to achieve unity, to create wholeness out of disparate pieces. The medium and the materials may be different, but what they seek is the same; they resonate with the same part of you."

CHEESE SPREADER
KELLY TOWNSEND

114

Photo by Amy Melious

KELLY TOWNSEND

Kelly Townsend moved to the hills of California early in the 1980s, and found himself living in a community of woodworkers. "I was not a woodworker myself at the time," Kelly remembers, "but I had a great appreciation for the kind of work these people were doing. One way I could share in the beauty they were creating was to buy spoons, which I gave away as gifts. The ones I liked best were made by Bill Chappelow, and his utensils have always been my inspiration." (Chappelow, whose work appears on pages 31, 32, 42, 44, 45, 88, 89, is one of the most influential American spoonmakers.)

"Not long afterward, I got to meet Bill in person. He was incredibly supportive, and the things he taught me were really helpful to my work. Bill brings such a high level of craftsmanship to everything he does, no matter how simple. In fact, I think it's the simplicity and functionality of utensils that appeals to me most. There's a real spiritual quality in being able to focus so completely on something so ordinary."

As Kelly began developing his own skills, he experimented with a number of objects, in addition to the spoons, stirrers, spreaders and spatulas he makes today.

"I don't much care for assembly, for putting things together. What I really like is the solidness of wood, so carving was a natural for me." One of his favorite projects was a large water dipper, fashioned from a wood called osage orange, or bodark, commissioned by a Native American medicine man for use in the traditional sweatlodge ceremonies.

FIVE-PIECE UTENSIL SET
KELLY TOWNSEND

The simple but practical shapes of these utensils are roughed out using the band saw and then the 6" x 48" belt sander, beginning with a 40-grit belt. Finer shaping and sanding of the surfaces is done on a pneumatic drum sander, with various grits, and the utensils (shown here in madrone) are oiled with mineral oil. The racks are produced by drilling $1/4$"-diameter holes, then gluing in 2" lengths of $1/4$" wooden dowel.

Photo by Bob Barrett

GINA CHAPLAIN

In addition to woodwork and silversmithing, Gina Chaplain's education has included study in painting, drawing, sculpture, and ceramics. This varied training has given her command of a number of materials and techniques, making it easy for her to enjoy one of her favorite creative activities: combining different materials, like the rosewood and silver of these butter knives and demitasse spoons.

Surprisingly, what led her to utensil making was not her education as an artist, but working in a restaurant as a cook. "My goal was to become a gourmet chef," Gina says, "but I discovered that I also liked food presentation, the way everything is arranged on the plate so that it has the most pleasing appearance. In fact, I wanted the entire table to look great. When we use things every day, why shouldn't they be beautiful?

"As part of my training as a silversmith, I knew a lot about making jewelry, and I applied those techniques to creating spoons and knives. Interestingly enough, I've found that I prefer making adornments that go with food — things you can use, handle, and touch — rather than adornments for the body. My mom calls my utensils 'jewels for the table.'"

Gina attributes the delightfully different squiggles of her utensil handles, so characteristic of her style, to one of her most important early influences, the books of Dr. Seuss. "It's important to me to portray a sense of playfulness and whimsy in my work, as well as elegance and a touch of fantasy."

SILVER & ROSEWOOD DEMITASSE & SPREADERS
GINA CHAPLAIN

Photo by Bob Barrett

GLENN ELVIG

Glenn Elvig's career as a craftsperson began in high school, when he and a ceramics teacher bought a kiln to produce functional stoneware. "I'd wanted to be an artist since I was four years old," Glenn recalls, "and I started out selling my pots in eleventh grade.

"After I got my degree in art education, I taught for a few years, but I soon realized that teaching art was no substitute for making art. I decided to quit teaching and open my own studio in Minneapolis."

Glenn's sculptural boxes and wall pieces were first exhibited at the American Craft Council's 1987 Winter Market in Baltimore, where they sold well. Three years later, at the ACC's Armory Show in New York, the response was overwhelming.

The napkin holders are offshoots of one of Glenn's favorite designs, his "Big Bopper" chair, which uses a massive coiled spring as its base. "I'm intrigued by the spring form, and I've begun to use it a lot in my designs," Glenn says. "I've started doing other tableware, and it's fun for me to create new functional work that preserves the design integrity of my larger pieces."

SPRING NAPKIN HOLDERS
GLENN ELVIG

Each napkin holder consists of a piece of $1/4$"-diameter steel rod, bent to a spiral and attached to a turned wood sphere. (For this set, Glenn used madrone, myrtlewood, maple and walnut.) The spheres are turned on the lathe as if they were spindles with only a single ball in the middle. A square of cardboard with a 3"-diameter hole, cut in half, serves as a sizing template. Each sphere begins as a 3" x 3" x 5" rectangular solid; during turning, a dowel-shaped nub is left on either end to keep the sphere attached to the lathe. The nubs are then band-sawed off and the ball sanded smooth. To make the spring, Glenn starts with a long steel rod (at least 3 feet in length, to allow for enough leverage to bend). He heats the rod and bends it around a fixed piece of 2"-diameter galvanized pipe. The spiral is then spray-painted and pressure-fit into a hole drilled into the wood.

ROSEWOOD PICNIC BOX
JANET & JAY O'ROURKE

ROSEWOOD PICNIC BOX
JANET & JAY O'ROURKE

In a project that combines the utensil maker's skill with the art of the boxmaker, Janet and Jay O'Rourke have designed the ultimate picnic set for two.

To make the box, Janet and Jay start with a solid block of rosewood, 2$\frac{1}{8}$" thick. Part C, the lid, is bandsawed off, and Part A, the body of the box, is routed to produce the empty interior, leaving a $\frac{1}{4}$"-thick bottom. The two ebony ends are rough shaped, and a hole is drilled in the inside face of each end, as well as the butt of the lid, to take the hinge pin. Once the interior surfaces are finish sanded, the box is assembled, including the lid.

PART	DESCRIPTION	DIMENSIONS	QUANTITY
A	Box Body	1$\frac{1}{2}$" x 5" x 8"	1
B	Box End	$\frac{5}{8}$" x 2$\frac{1}{2}$" x 5"	2
C	Lid	$\frac{1}{2}$" x 5" x 8"	1
D	Hinge Pin	$\frac{1}{16}$" x $\frac{1}{2}$"	2
E	Utensil Insert	1$\frac{1}{4}$" x 5" x 8"	1
F	Utensils	$\frac{1}{2}$" x 1" x 7"	6

Into the utensil insert, Part E, the shapes of the three utensils are cut using a jigsaw. The edges of these cuts may be cleaned up with a drum sander sleeve attached to the drill press. When complete, the insert simply fits into place; no glue is used to attach it.

The exterior of the box is now sanded on the belt sander using progressively finer grits. A drill bit is applied to the front edge of the box at an angle to rough out the thumb-hole depression under the lid, which is then filed, sanded, and polished. The box is given an oil finish, then buffed to high luster with wax on a buffing wheel.

The utensils themselves are bandsawed, then shaped, sanded, and oiled using the same techniques described on page 36. Note the delicate bevel detail the O'Rourkes have given to the ends of the fork and spoon handle.

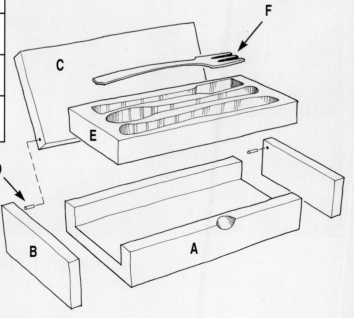

Photo by Bob Barrett

JANET & JAY O'ROURKE

Janet and Jay O'Rourke are masters at the art of transforming small pieces of intensely colored natural hardwoods into gemlike objects that are as practical as they are irresistible. "Our first picnic box was done in walnut," Janet recalls, "but over the years we've grown to prefer the rich color of rosewood, and that's what this one is made of." The picnic box includes knife, fork, and spoon service for four.

Through their woodworking company, Jay O'Boxes, the O'Rourkes handcraft boxes for everything from toothpicks to business cards to jewelry, but whatever its use, an O'Rourke box is eagerly sought by collectors. Their pieces are exhibited in shows and galleries throughout the country, including "A Celebration of the Creative Works of the Hand," the White House Christmas Tree, and the Sausalito Art Festival, where they were honored with a first-place award in 1994. Their work has appeared in a number of publications, and they were the subject of a recent feature article in *American Craft Magazine*.

"It takes an enormous amount of work to create a box that satisfies me," says Janet, "and sometimes I wonder why I work so hard. Then I remember my dreams, and the things I believe in and aspire to, and it all seems worthwhile again."

BAMBOO BASTING BRUSHES
KEITH LEBENZON

There are over a thousand species of bamboo, and the plant can be found growing wild or as a cultivated ornamental in many parts of the country. To make a pastry-brush or basting-brush handle, select a piece of bamboo up to $1/2$" in diameter with an appealing shape, and cut to desired length using a fine-toothed saw, to prevent splitting. If the bamboo is green or freshly harvested, let it air-dry for three months. Synthetic or animal hair is available from craft supply stores, and from shops that sell materials for freshwater fly-tying. Since these brushes will come in contact with food, make sure any nonsynthetic hair has been thoroughly washed and sterilized.

The hair is held in a tight bundle with thread and glued into the bamboo handle using a waterproof resin. When the resin is dry, the thread is removed and the brush can be shaped with scissors if desired. Treat the bamboo with carnauba or comparable wax to protect it from moisture.

Photo by Bob Barrett

KEITH LEBENZON

Keith Lebenzon was a college business major when he happened to take a class in ceramics. "The first day, when the instructor sat down at the potter's wheel and centered that clay, I was captivated," Keith remembers, "and from then on, I took every clay class I could. After graduation, I began making my living as a potter."

Keith got interested in brushes because he needed them to paint the glazes on his pots. "I kept wanting finer and finer brushes, but I just couldn't afford them. The best kind, from Japan and China, cost $90 apiece, and in 1970, that was the same as my monthly rent. It didn't occur to me to make my own brushes until one day I accidentally stepped on a store-bought one and the head came off.

"I had made a plant hanger out of some interestingly shaped bamboo I found in my neighbor's yard. I broke off a piece, and attached the brush head with some Elmer's glue. It worked so well that I began making my own, using local bamboo and goat hair I got from a nearby farm. Compared to pottery, the brushes were more fun to make. What's more, they didn't have to be fired in the kiln, where sometimes half my pots would break. When a friend entered them in a local craft competition and they won an award, I decided to turn to brushes full-time."

The handles of Keith's brushes are made from black bamboo, which he raises himself. "People's hands are all different," Keith says, "and I make my brushes short and long, fat and skinny, straighter and crookeder so there's a fit for everybody." The heads are pure animal hair, but Keith points out that no animals are harmed to make his brushes. "My favorite is Roosevelt elk, a protected species which is native to Oregon where I live, and the fur is a by-product."

KENTUCKY SPRINGS SALAD TONGS
KYLE ELLISON

Each set of tongs is hand-steamed and bent into shape until cool, to create the distinctive wood springs that keep the tongs open, and also allow them to fold flat. The woods used are cherry, oak, and walnut, and each is given a mineral-oil finish.

KYLE ELLISON

"I began woodworking with a totally blind woodworker, who taught me basic skills and provided a fully equipped shop. I learned that vision is but one of many important tools, and that the quality of a wood finish is judged as much by the hand as by the eye," says Kentuckian Kyle Ellison.

Working together as Kentucky Springs Woodworking, Kyle and his teacher, Jim Scoggins, have developed two simple but extremely useful and ingenious utensils: one-handed salad tongs, and a guitar-string cheese slicer. "I've tried to trace the origins of these tongs, but with no success so far," says Kyle. "I think the design may be very old."

The idea for the guitar-string cheese slicer came about when Kyle noticed that most such utensils have no provision for replacing the cutting wire. If it breaks, you have to buy another cheese slicer. So Kyle and Jim took advantage of the ready availability of steel acoustic guitar strings, which come with a button on one end.

"What motivates me is the challenge of designing useful household tools with moving parts. These pieces must be simple, durable, and beautiful. My goal is to build tools that work so well that the old tools are sent off to a yard sale," Kyle says. The partners make a point of working only in native hardwoods: "The Good Lord made the tree," observes Jim, "and we take pieces of it, and however it comes out, that's the way it's gonna be."

GUITAR-STRING CHEESE SLICER
KYLE ELLISON

These cheese slicers in cherry and walnut begin as 5" x 2½" x ⅜" rectangular blanks. The button end of the guitar string is anchored in a hole drilled in one corner of the slicer. The wire itself then runs through a smaller-diameter hole, across two posts that form it into a cutting edge, and then through a second hole to the tightening knob. All the parts are standard brass fittings, and the wood is finished in mineral oil.

RHETT ZOLL

"My interest in working with wood began when I was young; I spent as much time as I could in my father's workshop," says Rhett Zoll. Rhett's love of wood led him to earn a Bachelor of Fine Arts Degree in Furniture Design, and as these Zoll Woodworks utensils show, Rhett has put his knowledge to good use.

With his wife, Ronda, and brother, Russell, Rhett produces furniture, office accessories and gifts, as well as kitchen utensils and tableware. A series of whimsical baby rattles has just been introduced, shaped like ice-cream bars and ice-cream sandwiches. Their designs are exhibited and sold in shops and galleries throughout the country and were recently featured in a major exhibition in Tokyo.

Rhett's ability as a furniture designer has won him a number of important commissions, including executive office suites and an oversize gavel, presented to former Speaker of the United States House of Representatives Tip O'Neill. Rhett's articles on woodworking have been published in *The American Woodworker* and *Wood Magazine*, and he is active in local and national craft guilds and associations. In addition, he passes along his knowledge by teaching woodworking in his hometown of Goshen, New York.

STACKING CORK-LINED COASTERS
RHETT ZOLL

These octagonal coasters are milled from $\frac{1}{2}$" mahogany. A router is used to hollow the face, to which a $\frac{1}{8}$"-thick disc of cork is glued using waterproof adhesive. Four router cuts in the sides allow each coaster to fit on the stand, which is made from four pieces of $\frac{1}{4}$"-thick mahogany, joined at the base. The set is finished with a water-resistant polyurethane finish.

WALNUT, OAK & MAPLE
SALT & PEPPER SHAKERS
RHETT ZOLL

These salt and pepper shakers begin as 2"-square blocks of oak, 4" long. Each block is turned on edge, and a shallow $1/2$"-wide dado is milled on two edges to hold the $1/2$"-square contrasting wood legs. The oak blank is then sliced in two pieces, about $3/4$" long and $3^1/4$" long. The shorter piece, which becomes the removable shaker top, is drilled with a $1/16$" bit to produce the dispenser holes. The longer piece is drilled from above with a $1^1/4$"-diameter bit to make a 2"-deep cavity to hold the salt or pepper. To assemble, the legs are glued to the shaker body, but not to the top, which is held in place by a slight pressure fit. Prior to assembly, sand all parts, and make sure the top fits tightly enough to stay in place, but can still be removed when necessary to fill the shaker.

COOLING RACK
RHETT ZOLL

For this cooling rack, 7" and 14" lengths of $1/2$"-square maple are turned on their edges and glued into shallow triangular dados, milled into the $3/4$" x 1" walnut feet, using waterproof adhesive. The rack, which can also be used as a hot plate or trivet, is then given a mineral-oil finish.

MAPLE VERTIZONTAL
DENNIS ELLIOTT
132

DENNIS ELLIOTT

Dennis Elliott first began turning wood 20 years ago and has been a full-time professional since 1987. "My work consists mainly of large vessels that are turned on the lathe and accented with carving. I like to give these pieces a tactile feel. On some, I incorporate multiple woods or materials like molten pewter, Avonite, or semiprecious stones. Bleaching or burning the wood can also add interest."

As a young man growing up in London, England, however, woodwork was only a hobby for Dennis. He was a professional rock musician, the drummer for a band called Foreigner, whose hit songs from the 1970s and '80s are still played on classic rock stations. "In creating music, you're creating out of thin air," Dennis observes. "There's no material that you're working with when you begin. But with a solid object like a piece of a tree, you can only do it once. The responsibility is therefore greater than creating a new song, which can be wiped out and started again.

"After 10 years of rock and roll, I was ready to leave the band, though I've kept involved in a few music projects," Dennis says. "Over the past few years, my focus in wood turning seems to have lingered on making these pieces that are so interesting to touch and that have the look of stonework. Some have abstract markings on them and appear to be of ancient or Indian inspiration. Since I never studied anything like that, I guess I just like the effect!"

The table piece shown represents an early stage in the transformation which Dennis has been making toward purely sculptural wall pieces. These "vertizontals," as he calls them, are eagerly sought by collectors, and are in the permanent collections of the Renwick Gallery of the Smithsonian Institute in Washington, the American Craft Museum, and the Boston Museum of Fine Arts.

"Playing music onstage is instantaneous. Any movement you make is done and gone; it's just a feeling at that time," Dennis explains. "But with wood, the vessel I turn will probably outlive me."

TORTILLA ROLLER
NICK COOK

This basic rolling pin is one of the simplest and most useful kitchen utensils. After the form is turned on the lathe, the ends are cut off and sanded round and smooth.

NICK COOK

"I grew up around my father's woodworking equipment," says woodturner Nick Cook. "In fact, my father jokes that I started woodworking when I was tall enough to see over the table saw." Although his career has included custom furniture design, starting a furniture manufacturing company, and sophisticated national sales and marketing positions, Nick's first love is wood turning.

"I find turning to be the most spontaneous and gratifying aspect of woodworking. You can see your form taking shape, and you quickly have a completed work. Best of all, the only tool you need is a lathe."

Nick's reputation as one of the country's best-known turners began with his cocobolo wine bottle stoppers. "I enjoy turning artistic, one-of-a-kind pieces, but it's the functional work, like my wine stoppers, that allows me the luxury of doing that. To be successful, you need a product mix and a price mix — something to attract all types of buyers."

Over the years, the products of Nick's lathe have played an important part in increasing public interest in functional woodwork throughout the country. Perhaps even more important, Nick's know-how — and his willingness to share it through articles, seminars, lectures and workshops — have instructed and inspired countless up-and-coming woodworkers.

HONEY DIPPERS
NICK COOK

Nick uses close-grained hardwoods such as cherry, maple and walnut for these honey dippers. After turning on the lathe, the slots in the ends are cut on the band saw and the finished piece is oiled with mineral oil.

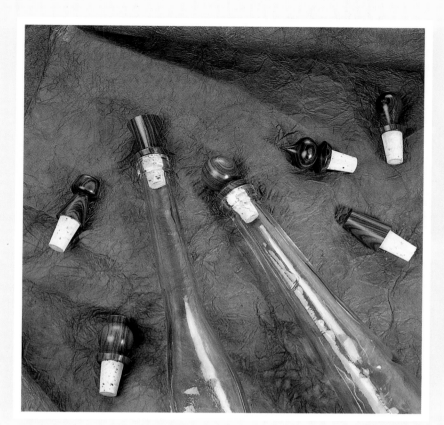

COCOBOLO WINE STOPPERS
NICK COOK

Nick uses a lathe attachment known as a machinist's collet chuck to turn $1\frac{1}{2}$"-square pieces of cocobolo for his wine stoppers. (The process is described in detail in "Collet Chuck Turning," an article Nick wrote in the May/June 1992 issue of *The Woodworker's Journal*.) The cork is specially constructed with a reinforcing dowel attached to the stopper.

POTATO MASHER
NICK COOK

An essential tool for the serious mashed-potato chef, this masher has a walnut handle and a head of ash. The handle is turned with a tenon; the hole in the head that will receive the tenon is bored prior to turning.

TEA SERVICE
STEVE GRAY & KATE NOBLE

Photo by Bob Barrett

STEVE GRAY & KATE NOBLE

Steve Gray and Kate Noble have always had a penchant for the unusual. "I studied photography in school," Steve recalls, "but when I got out of school I started making spinning wheels. Someone asked me to make one, and it wasn't long before I was designing my own. I went on to do some cabinetry and furniture, and then for almost 10 years I made kaleidoscopes."

Steve became well known for his unusual kaleidoscopes, many of which were sculptural as well as functional. "I like to do sculpture, because it gives me a way to find expression for myself. But for most people, pure sculpture is too hard to focus on. There's a need for some kind of anchor in functionality. The kaleidoscopes were a great way to combine the two."

Boxes, jars and screw-top containers are some of the other objects to which Steve and Kate have applied their design and woodworking talents. "Then someone asked us to make a tea set— another form that combines the sculptural with at least the idea of the functional." The set shown here is maple burl and ebony, and sits on its own tray, paved with blocks of burl.

CEREMONIAL GOBLETS
BETTY SCARPINO

Photo by Casalini

BETTY SCARPINO

"I guess you could say I fell into woodworking by accident," says Betty Scarpino, one of the country's leading woodturners. "While I was in graduate school, the company I worked for gave me the opportunity to take a few classes. It just so happened that the only classes I could take at night were math and woodworking. I liked woodworking so much that later on, when I was able to complete my education, I chose Industrial Arts as my major."

Betty started out making cutting boards, platters, and furniture, and her career got its first boost when she and a group of fellow artists joined together in a cooperative gallery in Columbia, Missouri. After Betty left Columbia, her former associates went on to form Bluestem Missouri Crafts, a gallery that continues to feature her work.

"I've always liked to work with my hands," Betty observes, "and I found that I especially liked turning on the lathe." Although she didn't commit to a career in wood turning until 1982, by 1990 she had been named editor-in-chief of *American Woodturner Magazine*, published by the American Association of Woodturners. Her work has won numerous awards, and she is much in demand for wood turning seminars and demonstrations in the United States and Canada.

"When I teach wood turning, I stress the importance of the basics. Once you've mastered the techniques of turning, then comes the fun part, exploring your own shapes and ideas." Having achieved such technical mastery, it's clear that exploration is where Betty is headed: "When I grow up," she says, "I want to be a sculptor."

CEREMONIAL GOBLETS &
SILVER ANNIVERSARY GOBLETS

These goblets are turned on the lathe from peach, walnut and maple. Betty has used a two-part chemical bleach to create the lightened areas. For the bead on the peach goblets, bleach is applied with a cotton swab; a cloth was used for the larger maple goblets. The irregular gouging on the sides of the walnut pair was done by hand with a chisel after the goblets were turned. All were finished in mineral oil.

Although these goblets are functional, Betty thinks that they are best suited for ceremonial use. Because they are white, the maple pair would be ideal for a wedding. Being made of wood, they can re-appear as the couple celebrates their fifth anniversary, and again at their twenty-fifth, because of the silver bead.

SAFETY TIP: When using chemical bleach, follow manufacturer's instructions. Always wear eye protection and rubber gloves, and work in a properly ventilated area.

SILVER ANNIVERSARY GOBLETS
BETTY SCARPINO

METRIC EQUIVALENCE CHART

MM-Millimetres   CM-Centimetres

INCHES TO MILLIMETRES AND CENTIMETRES

INCHES	MM	CM	INCHES	CM	INCHES	CM
⅛	3	0.3	9	22.9	30	76.2
¼	6	0.6	10	25.4	31	78.7
½	13	1.3	12	30.5	33	83.8
⅝	16	1.6	13	33.0	34	86.4
¾	19	1.9	14	35.6	35	88.9
⅞	22	2.2	15	38.1	36	91.4
1	25	2.5	16	40.6	37	94.0
1¼	32	3.2	17	43.2	38	96.5
1½	38	3.8	18	45.7	39	99.1
1¾	44	4.4	19	48.3	40	101.6
2	51	5.1	20	50.8	41	104.1
2½	64	6.4	21	53.3	42	106.7
3	76	7.6	22	55.9	43	109.2
3½	89	8.9	23	58.4	44	111.8
4	102	10.2	24	61.0	45	114.3
4½	114	11.4	25	63.5	46	116.8
5	127	12.7	26	66.0	47	119.4
6	152	15.2	27	68.6	48	121.9
7	178	17.8	28	71.1	49	124.5
8	203	20.3	29	73.7	50	127.0

YARDS TO METRES

YARDS	METRES	YARDS	METRES	YARDS	METRES	YARDS	METRES	YARDS	METRES
⅛	0.11	2⅛	1.94	4⅛	3.77	6⅛	5.60	8⅛	7.43
¼	0.23	2¼	2.06	4¼	3.89	6¼	5.72	8¼	7.54
⅜	0.34	2⅜	2.17	4⅜	4.00	6⅜	5.83	8⅜	7.66
½	0.46	2½	2.29	4½	4.11	6½	5.94	8½	7.77
⅝	0.57	2⅝	2.40	4⅝	4.23	6⅝	6.06	8⅝	7.89
¾	0.69	2¾	2.51	4¾	4.34	6¾	6.17	8¾	8.00
⅞	0.80	2⅞	2.63	4⅞	4.46	6⅞	6.29	8⅞	8.12
1	0.91	3	2.74	5	4.57	7	6.40	9	8.23
1⅛	1.03	3⅛	2.86	5⅛	4.69	7⅛	6.52	9⅛	8.34
1¼	1.14	3¼	2.97	5¼	4.80	7¼	6.63	9¼	8.46
1⅜	1.26	3⅜	3.09	5⅜	4.91	7⅜	6.74	9⅜	8.57
1½	1.37	3½	3.20	5½	5.03	7½	6.86	9½	8.69
1⅝	1.49	3⅝	3.31	5⅝	5.14	7⅝	6.97	9⅝	8.80
1¾	1.60	3¾	3.43	5¾	5.26	7¾	7.09	9¾	8.92
1⅞	1.71	3⅞	3.54	5⅞	5.37	7⅞	7.20	9⅞	9.03
2	1.83	4	3.66	6	5.49	8	7.32	10	9.14

INDEX